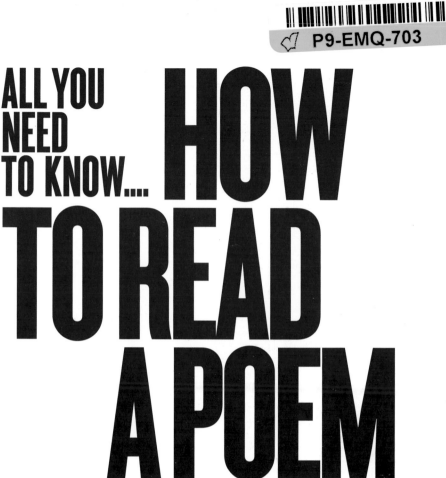

ALL YOU NEED TO KNOW....

HOW TO READ A POEM

BY MALCOLM HEBRON

WITH ANDREW HODGSON

AND CAROLINE MOORE

CONTENTS

To Victòria, plena de seny

INTRODUCTION: LISTENING TO GHOSTS

I've never seen a ghost. But there's a house I know in Devon which used to be a barn. One day the owner went downstairs and found a man standing there, in Victorian clothes. He was just standing, lost in thought, in the middle of the kitchen. After a time, without a word, the visitor left.

So I'm quite willing to accept there may be ghosts out there. I've just never seen one myself. But I have, in one way, had many meetings with the dead, and you have too: through reading books.

It's easy to forget what strange things books *are*. The shelf I'm looking at, right now, holds the words of human beings from all sorts of times and places: just by opening these volumes, I can let their voices flood into my mind. I can share the experiences of a soldier in the First

World War, listen to someone who was in love in the 16th century, lose myself in a story that takes me to the taverns of 17th-century Spain. Through their writings, authors from all places and ages have sent their experiences out into the world where, miraculously, they have survived, while the writers themselves have lived their lives and passed on. And the most distilled, intense record they have left us is to be found in poetry.

Let's go back to my ghost story from Devon. But now imagine it's *you* who goes downstairs. There in front of you, in flickering candlelight, is an old man, dressed in Victorian clothes. He has white hair. He leans on a stick. The room is quite bare, but there's a tall mirror in front of him. He stares into it for a while. You stand, transfixed. Then he starts speaking – to you, or to himself? Has he even seen you? It's hard to tell. His voice is quiet, almost a whisper.

This is what he says:

> I look into my glass,
> And view my wasting skin
> And say, 'Would God it came to pass
> My heart had shrunk as thin!'
>
> For then I, undistrest
> By hearts grown cold to me
> Could lonely wait my endless rest
> With equanimity.
>
> But Time, to make me grieve,
> Part steals, lets part abide;
> And shakes this fragile frame at eve
> With throbbings of noontide.

Then a long silence falls. The candle sputters and goes out. Not knowing how, you find yourself outside. But the words of the old man stay with you.

> *I'm getting old,* he seemed to be saying, *my skin is wasting away, my body is frail. If only my feelings would fade away as well! Then I wouldn't mind if people felt coldly towards me, for I could just wait calmly for death to come. But no, Time won't let me off the hook. Still I feel the passions and desires that I did when I was a young man in the noon of life, surging through me. I'm old on the outside, but young on the inside, close to death yet still so alive. Why can't my feelings go away and leave me in peace?*

It's a sad thought – the shadows are lengthening... Is that what it's like being old? Some of what he says seems odd, and surprising.

> And view my wasting skin.

Curious words. Why *view*, and not *see*? A *view* suggests you're having a good long look, like the view from a clifftop. And *wasting*, not *wasted*: that *–ing*, that little word ending, makes us think that the skin is wasting away, *right now, even as he looks in the mirror.*

And the *fragile frame* is presumably the man's body, yet it makes you think of some tottering wooden barn, shaken by *throbbings of noontide*, as if his feelings are like a wind or an earthquake stirring the foundations, making the whole structure creak. The poet doesn't sound as if he is feeling sorry for himself, though. His verses are delivered in a dignified, unhurried way, through lines of measured rhyming verse, with some thoughtful, educated words, such as *equanimity*. That's not how we sound when we're asking for sympathy. There is no complaint here, just a restrained statement of feeling.

> For then I, undistrest...

Undistrest is another unusual word: the life the poet dreams of is one defined by its absence of distress rather than by any positive quality. And look at that word the poem ends on: *noontide.* In the Bible noontide was associated with temptation: Christian monks used to talk about the *noontide demon.* You don't need to know this to understand the poem, but the poet clearly knew it, and his image is carefully chosen. This is a poem about a particular kind of temptation: the temptation of youthful desire and passion.

Well, that is one way of reading a poem: attending to the words that surprise you and asking yourself why they're there. On this occasion you met the ghost of the poet and novelist, Thomas Hardy.

Another way of reading a poem is to see it as a *journey.* It takes us from the familiar to the strange, from the known to the unknown. In the verses we have looked at, Hardy takes us on a journey from looking into a mirror – a familiar experience – to what must be for most of us the unknown, strange world of being old yet flooded with the passions of youth.

Some poems, especially from earlier history, sound rather grand, as if a wizard or prophet is speaking. A lot of modern poetry is more like someone speaking to you across the table. But in both cases – whether it's the prophet speaking, or the companion across the table – a poem makes you put other things to the back of your mind and *give the speaker your attention.*

That's what this book is about. Its aim is to give you some suggestions on how we can pay attention to poetry, and make the most of its message. "It is the business of the poet to touch our hearts by showing his own," was how Thomas Hardy put it. The pages that follow are about how to be touched. How to read a poem. How to listen to ghosts.

SECTION

WHAT'S IT ALL ABOUT

"The poets have been mysteriously silent on the subject of cheese."   (G K Chesterton)

When we read a poem for the first time, a useful thing to do is *to forget it's a poem*. We need to be clear *what* it is saying before we think about *how* it is saying it. (There are poems about all sorts of things though not many, as Chesterton reminds us, on the subject of cheese.)

Love and Friendship

Love is like the wild rose briar,
Friendship, like the holly tree –

The holly is dark when the rose-briar blooms
But which will bloom most constantly?

The wild rose-briar is sweet in spring,
Its summer blossoms scent the air;
Yet wait till winter comes again
And who will call the wild-briar fair?

Then scorn the silly rose-wreath now
And deck thee with the holly's sheen,
That when December blights thy brow
He still may leave thy garland green.

(Emily Brontë, 1818-1848)

In other words...

*Love is like a rose, and friendship is like the holly. Next to the
blooming rose, the holly seems dull. But which one would you rely on?
In spring and summer, the rose is in bloom and smells lovely. But in
winter it fades away. Forget about love, then, which is wonderful
but short-lived, and go for friendship. Then, when your winter time
comes, you still have a friend you can count on.*

Or, to put it in a sentence: *romantic love is wonderful but short-lived,
while friendship is permanent and won't desert you.*

You might ask: "Why didn't she just say that and save us all some
time?" But Brontë has put these thoughts across in a way which is
musical, which moves in a pleasant rhythmic way, and gives us pictures
to go with the abstract ideas. All of this helps us to remember it.
Another poet, W. H. Auden, defined poetry simply as "memorable
speech".

The paraphrase above is what we call the **argument** of the poem.

Once we have an idea of the argument, we can ask: "What does it make us think about?" The poem above turns our mind to love and friendship, but maybe to other things, too – how so often in life the most exciting things only last for a short time, while the most valuable ones are those we don't pay much attention to.

The subjects that a poem makes us think about are its **themes**. It's a common misconception that the ideas of poetry are deep: often they are quite simple and familiar. But Brontë expresses what is a familiar idea in a vivid, striking way and in so doing she makes the familiar seem unfamiliar. Another famous remark about poetry is that it gives us (in the words of Alexander Pope) "What oft was thought but ne'er so well expressed".

Let's look at a harder poem. Emily Brontë led us by the hand and pointed out what her images meant. But not all poets do this. Sometimes they give us more work to do. Here's another poem about a rose.

The Sick Rose

O Rose thou art sick.
The invisible worm,
That flies in the night
In the howling storm:

Has found out thy bed
Of crimson joy:
And his dark secret love
Does thy life destroy.

(William Blake, 1757-1827)

Where Brontë kindly told us what the rose and holly stood for, Blake is not so considerate. So all we can do is retell the strange little story:

> *You're ill, rose! There's a worm, which is invisible and flies in the stormy night and it's found you in your bed and it's destroying you with its love.*

So what do the rose and the worm mean? I don't know. *No one knows.* Critics and scholars still debate these mysterious eight lines. And Blake didn't help us by writing down the answer on the back. Perhaps even *he* didn't know! Maybe it was a vision or dream that he just wrote down because it felt significant to him.

A rose is associated in our minds with love, beauty, fragility (as in the previous poem). And it's clear that the worm here is something dangerous – it's invisible, it flies in a storm, it destroys with a *secret love.* Could it be one of those insects that gets into flowers and makes them ill and covered in spots? Maybe. But the poet is not writing an article for a gardening magazine. He must have bigger ideas in mind.

What, then, does the poem make us think about? Perhaps of how vulnerable, beautiful things are open to attack, how even love can be damaging. Perhaps *dark secret* suggests the wrong kind of love? When we learn that the poem is from a collection called *Songs of Innocence and Experience*, we might find that useful, too. The rose is like youthful innocence, and the worm, maybe, is the forces of experience that come for us when we grow up, that eat away our innocence. Some critics have even suggested that the poem refers to sex – the worm, the crimson bed… Perhaps they're right.

'The Sick Rose' is an example of a poem which on one level is a story of a flower and a worm. But we suspect it's really about something else, just as the fable of the hare and the tortoise isn't about the different velocity of animals but about how sure and steady wins the day over sheer speed.

Often, in poetry, things or animals or plants stand for ideas: a rose for love, holly for friendship, a worm for corruption. When used in this way, they are called **symbols**. Symbols can be an effective way of helping us understand the invisible world of ideas.

STIRRING UP OUR EMOTIONS

Poems convey *emotions* – hope, despair, defiance, love, fear. It's hard really to separate the mind and the heart. The main two uses we make of language are to say what we think and to say (or show) what we feel. Poetry brings the two together. Robert Frost puts it like this: "Poetry is when an emotion has found its thought and the thought has found words." Here's a poem by a writer who had a lot to say about emotions, William Wordsworth.

I wandered lonely as a cloud

I wandered lonely as a cloud
That floats on high o'er vales and hills,

When all at once I saw a crowd,
A host, of golden daffodils;
Beside the lake, beneath the trees,
Fluttering and dancing in the breeze.

Continuous as the stars that shine
And twinkle on the milky way,
They stretched in never-ending line
Along the margin of a bay:
Ten thousand saw I at a glance,
Tossing their heads in sprightly dance.

The waves beside them danced; but they
Outdid the sparkling waves in glee:
A poet could not but be gay,
In such a jocund company:
I gazed – and gazed – but little thought
What wealth the show to me had brought:

For oft, when on my couch I lie
In vacant or in pensive mood,
They flash upon that inward eye
Which is the bliss of solitude;
And then my heart with pleasure fills,
And dances with the daffodils.

(William Wordsworth, 1770-1850)

This is a famous poem, but the best thing to do with a famous poem is to pretend you're the first person who's ever seen it. Imagine it's just tumbled out of a dusty box in a charity shop. Read it like that and you might be surprised. Is this about the poet in ecstasy at the beauty of daffodils? That's what we might *expect* in a poem which begins as this one does (and indeed the poem is often, wrongly, called 'Daffodils').

But poets love confounding our expectations, and when we read a poem we have to be careful to attend to what it is *actually* saying. In terms of feeling, then, what is going on? First the speaker says he *wandered lonely*. There's our first emotion word, *lonely*, but he doesn't *sound* very lonely: it comes over as a rather nice loneliness, floating freely like a cloud. Then he sees the daffodils. Look at the wonderfully inventive verbs and adverbs: *fluttering, twinkling, tossing...* They *outdid the sparkling waves in glee...* He tells us that the company of the flowers made him feel gay, in its sense of "happy":

> A poet could not but be gay.

But as he loses himself in *looking*, he doesn't think at all about the experience:

> I gazed – and gazed – but little thought
> What wealth the show to me had brought.

The sight is doing him good without him even noticing. It's not until the last verse that the joy catches up with him, as a delayed reaction. When he's idle and *pensive*, the daffodils come back to him as a golden memory and

> ... then my heart with pleasure fills,
> And dances with the daffodils...

Far from being the word *daffodils*, that little word *then*, in the second last line, is perhaps the most important in the poem. It is the word on which the poems turns. His heart dances with the daffodils *now*, in a way it *didn't* dance with them first time round. (*I gazed – and gazed – but little thought…*)

So the poem takes us on a much more interesting emotional journey than we might expect from the opening lines. As one of the best modern critics of Wordsworth, Seamus Perry, says, this is really a poem about "sitting on your sofa" – a poem about memory. Wordsworth is telling us that the happiest moments in life sometimes go unnoticed at the time; we're so busy living them, experiencing them, that we're not really aware of being happy, or full of wonder. Only later do these moments come back to us – as intense memories – and it is then that we feel the pleasure or wonder we didn't really feel at the time.

"Poetry is the language in which man explores his own amazement," said Christopher Fry, and it is worth noting that the word *amazement* suggests not only wonder but also bewilderment or confusion – the maze of feelings and thoughts that the poet must work through, as Wordsworth does in "I wandered lonely as a cloud".

His poem is what we call a **lyric**, the most common type of poetry nowadays. Lyrics tend to be short and compressed – little grenades of thought-feeling-words. When they are in the first person, with an "I" speaking to us, they will often tell us directly what emotions are involved: *lonely... gay... bliss... pleasure.*

But there are other kinds of poem, and emotion can be conveyed in other ways. Here's a less well-known piece, a description of a bird that perches in a crocodile's mouth and acts as an avian toothpick, pecking food from between its teeth:

The Crocodile Bird

Beside the fruitful shore of muddy Nile,
Upon a sunny bank outstretchèd lay
In monstrous length, a mighty Crocodile,
That crammed with guiltless blood, and greedy prey
Of wretched people travailling that way,

Thought all things less than his disdainful pride.
I saw a little bird, called Tedula,
The least of thousands which on earth abide,
That forced this hideous beast to open wide
The grisly gates of his devouring hell,
And let him feed, as Nature doth provide,
Upon his jaws, that with black venom swell.
Why then should greatest things the least disdain,
Since that so small so mighty can constrain?

(Edmund Spenser, 1552-1599.
From *Visions of the World's Vanity*)

In these lines Spenser gives us an interesting little tale of how a mighty monster can be controlled by a tiny little bird, who forces it to open its jaws and let him peck away at the scraps. And he wraps it up with a moral: big powerful animals shouldn't think they are so great, when tiny ones can sometimes control them. He probably meant us to think about kings and popes and the common man, using the animal story to make his point. This particular kind of tale is called a **fable**.

But at the same time the poet winds us into his world on the banks of the sunny Nile by making us feel things. Horrible monster! Poor travellers! Plucky little bird! We take it all in much better if we're emotionally involved.

How does he achieve this? Look, first, at the words he uses to make the crocodile seem violent and unpleasant: *monstrous, greedy, disdainful, hideous*. Even the bits of the crocodile, like the *black venom* on his teeth, are nasty. This kind of language is called **emotive**. Emotive language goes straight for the jugular, stirring up our feelings. Meanwhile, the bird, the *tedula*, is *little... the least of thousands*. We admire him as a cunning little chappy, forcing the mighty beast to open its jaws. Other emotive words make us feel sorry for the travellers, who are *guiltless*

and *wretched*. We react not just to the **meanings** of words, but also to their **associations**. For example, *black* literally means a colour, but in the phrase *black venom* we associate it with death and evil.

The second way the poet is swaying our emotions is by the use of images. First we see the Nile as a pleasant place, with a *fruitful shore* and *sunny bank*. Those pictures of fruit and sun conjure up a picture of a placid and fertile place. But it is spoilt by the huge monster. His mouth is pictured as *grisly gates*, leading to *devouring hell*, and his jaws drip with *black venom*.

Finally, a poet can use *sound* to nudge us into imagining the scene more vividly and getting emotionally involved. Just listen to that fantastic line

That crammed with guiltless blood, and greedy prey.

It's crammed itself with juicy sounds that echo the monster crunching up its victims: *crammed, **guiltless** ... **greedy***. Now contrast these heavy monster sounds with the light tripping sounds around the tiny bird:

I saw a little bird, called Tedula.

Those heavy sounds come back to give us the big, dangerous *grisly gates*, and the stressed *black venom swell*. This is like background music to a film, taking our emotions this way and that.

CHAPTER 3

LOOKING FOR CONFLICT

One helpful tip is to look for the central tension, or opposition, in a poem. The German poet Goethe said: "out of the quarrel with ourselves we make poetry". As readers, we can try to trace those quarrels in the poetry we read.

Think about the poems we have read so far. All of them are working out some kind of opposition. Hardy's poem, "I look into my glass", describes the tension between the ageing body and the still virile feelings within. Emily Brontë explores the opposition between romantic love – sensational but brief – and friendship. Blake's 'The Sick Rose' is about the opposition between the rose and the worm, innocence and corruption.

The opposition in Wordsworth's poem is less obvious, but it involves a kind of tension between an event when we *experience* it and later, when we *remember* it, a tension between the *then* and the *now*. Spenser's concern is the opposition between the mighty crocodile and the tiny bird which controls him. In each case, there's a kind of either/or – an on the one hand/on the other hand working itself out.

And what is true of these poems is true of most poetry. There is almost always an opposition – between positive and negative, good and evil, order and disorder, love and death, pleasant and unpleasant. It might be buried deep or it might be on the surface. It is often there at the start: *O Rose, thou art sick!* Beauty versus sickness. Everything follows from that.

Read this poem by Lord Byron and see if you can find opposing words or ideas early on.

She Walks in Beauty

> She walks in beauty, like the night
> Of cloudless climes and starry skies;
> And all that's best of dark and bright
> Meet in her aspect and her eyes;
> Thus mellowed to that tender light
> Which heaven to gaudy day denies.
>
> One shade the more, one ray the less,
> Had half impaired the nameless grace
> Which waves in every raven tress,
> Or softly lightens o'er her face;
> Where thoughts serenely sweet express,
> How pure, how dear their dwelling-place.
>
> And on that cheek, and o'er that brow,
> So soft, so calm, yet eloquent,

The smiles that win, the tints that glow,
But tell of days in goodness spent,
A mind at peace with all below,
A heart whose love is innocent!

The central tension in this poem is there from the very first line. It is between light and dark: she, the poet's subject, walks in *beauty*, like the *night*. It is the stars that give the night its beauty. The beautiful woman brings together the night and the stars:

all that's best of dark and bright
Meet in her aspect, and her eyes.

She embodies a *tender light*, the day mellowed by the night. She occupies the perfect middle point, one more *shade* or one more *ray* would spoil it. The beauty is in her dark *raven* hair, and *lightens* in her face. In the final stanza this physical beauty becomes a picture of moral perfection, as light and dark give way to an other-worldly *heart whose love is innocent*. The beautiful woman herself has worked out the opposition of light and dark, forming a mysterious harmony.

Here, by way of contrast, is a poem by one of my favourite contemporary poets, Alice Oswald.

Body

This is what happened
the dead were settling in under their mud roof
and something was shuffling overhead

it was a badger treading on the thin partition

bewildered were the dead

going about their days and nights in the dark
putting their feet down carefully and finding themselves
floating
but that badger

still with the simple heavy box of his body needing to be
lifted
was shuffling away alive

hard at work
with the living shovel of himself
into the lane he dropped
    not once looking up

and missed the sight of his own corpse falling like a suitcase
towards him
with the grin like an opened zip
    (as I found it this morning)

and went on running with that bindweed will of his
went on running along the hedge and into the earth again
trembling
as if in a broken jug for one backwards moment
    water might keep its shape

    (Alice Oswald, from *Falling Awake*)

There is so much to enjoy here, from that startling opening picture of the dead settling in, to that wonderful comparison of the badger's will to bindweed. The poem creates a rich and vivid world for us to inhabit.

Is there a controlling opposition, helping to unite the various parts? I would suggest it's a very ancient opposition between the primal forces of life and death. On the one hand we have the dead, settling down, and on the other the living badger, shuffling away, going about his badgery business.

The tension runs through the language: the dead are *putting their feet down carefully* and *floating*, and these light and ethereal actions contrast with the badger with his *heavy body*. They, the dead, are *settled down* and he is *hard at work*. The opposition works itself out in the final lines, where the badger seems to be dead and alive at the same time, perhaps in his last *backwards moment* imagining scurrying along the hedge as he crashes down into the lane, where the poet finds him later.

In "Body" the central opposition is fairly straightforward; in the famous verses which follow it is much less so.

A Red, Red Rose

O my Luve's like a red, red rose,
That's newly sprung in June:
O my Luve's like a melodie,
That's sweetly played in tune.

As fair art thou, my bonnie lass,
So deep in luve am I;
And I will luve thee still, my dear,
Till a' the seas gang dry.

Till a' the seas gang dry, my dear,
And the rocks melt wi' the sun;
And I will luve thee still, my dear,
While the sands o' life shall run.

And fare-thee-weel, my only Luve!
And fare-thee-weel, a while!
And I will come again, my Luve,
Tho 'twere ten thousand mile.

(Robert Burns, 1759-1796)

This is one of the great romantic poems. Notice how Burns expresses an abstract idea by using a vivid concrete picture. His love is

like a red, red rose,
That's newly sprung in June.

That repeated *red* suggests how intense his passion is, and the idea of the rose being *newly sprung* gets across his sense of delighted surprise. His beloved is like a melody, not just *sweetly played* but *in tune* as well – double bonus! But the picture of music also stirs our imagination, and gets across the idea of him taking *time* to contemplate her, as it takes time to listen to a piece of music.

Later we have the images of the sea going dry, the rocks melting with the sun – images of impossible things, emphasising how he will love her forever. But they also put the idea of the end of time, and the end of love, in our minds. If we're looking for an internal tension here, it is between the rapture of the moment and the sense that it will not last, that time marches on. The big abstract word in the poem is *Luve*, but it's the concrete imagery that gives it depth and power.

The very images Burns uses suggest the tension at the heart of the poem, the tension between his knowledge that love can't last and his desperate hope that it will. In one sense that inspired word *sprung* isn't quite right: rosebushes *don't* spring up in June, they're there all year round. But roses *do* bloom in June. So the image is both natural and unnatural at the same time, both realistic and magical.

As anyone who knows about Burns's life will tell you, the truth was that he was a serial womaniser who was constantly falling in love and constantly thinking it would last for ever. But we don't need to know this biographical detail to feel the psychological truth of the poem. Every time you fall in love you think: this is it. And though Burns knows in one part of his mind that his love won't last for ever – *Till a' the seas gang dry* – he passionately believes that it will. The tone of the poem is an irresistible mixture of celebration and defiance.

John Donne's poem, 'The Sun Rising', begins with a surprising, even bewildering, series of images.

> Busy old fool, unruly Sun,
> Why dost thou thus,
> Through windows, and through curtains call on us?
> Must to thy motions lovers' seasons run?
> Saucy pedantic wretch, go chide
> Late school-boys, and sour prentices,
> Go tell Court-huntsmen, that the King will ride,
> Call country ants to harvest offices;
> Love, all alike, no season knows, nor clime,
> Nor hours, days, months, which are the rags of time.

AMBIGUITY

Poems are often ambiguous. It is possible to interpret them in different ways. In his "Elegy in a County Churchyard", Thomas Gray writes:

Full many a gem of purest ray serene
The dark, unfathomed caves of ocean bear;
Full many a flower is born to blush unseen
And waste its sweetness on the desert air.

Gray is telling us that people from poor backgrounds find it difficult to be famous. He compares them to gems, hidden away in caves, and to flowers which bloom in the desert instead of being plucked and displayed in vases.

The critic William Empson, however, says that while farm labourers may *want* to escape their poverty, gems *don't mind* being hidden in caves and flowers, surely, are quite happy to be left to *blush unseen*.

Besides, the verse is so beautiful that we might feel, on reading it, that this a perfectly healthy, happy state of existence. Why would we want to see it altered? The poet is suggesting the poor should not be denied the limelight. Yet the imagery of the gems and flowers seems to be at odds with the argument it is supposed to be supporting.

John Donne (1572 – 1631)

Donne's poetry is often like this: vehement, argumentative, with urgent commands and questions and words thrown almost violently together. (In Donne's poems, says one of his most observant critics, John Carey, words are packed in "like boulders".) The tone is dismissive but the images jump off the page.

Saucy pedantic wretch, go chide

The phrase *Saucy pedantic wretch* wittily combines two more or less opposite ideas – the sun as *pedantic* (inflexible, literal-minded, always correcting) yet *saucy* (its intrusions into the bedroom being bawdy and rude). Then come two short, forceful verbs: *go chide.* The conflict is clear: the sun is presented as a *negative* image, love as a *positive* one.

Donne makes us see the sun in an entirely new way. Normally we think of it as warm and comforting, a source of light and life – something essential to our happiness. Yet here it is a *fool, unruly, pedantic* and *saucy*, while love is elevated as knowing *no season... nor clime.* The opposition in the poem is between love on the one hand and the sun on the other.

So this is a poem which wittily stands not just the sun but one of the central images of poetry on its head. As John Peck says in his useful book, *How to Study a Poet*, light is usually associated with goodness or pleasure in poetry, dark with the opposite. Poets often set love against "the gloomy waste of existence", but it is daringly original to set it against the sun which "orders and organises" our lives.

Donne's poems restlessly play with ideas, making it unwise to form a judgement about them before we reach the last line: in this case, the speaker develops the opposition between sun and love before finally, and with unexpected tenderness, resolving the conflict by urging the sun to stay with him and the girl and warm them. It's as if poems like this are being worked on even while we read them, says John Carey:

> They have a recent, experimental feel, like a stretch of new road, where you have to edge past tar boilers and gravel lorries and men leaning on spades. Effort is still in the air, and the surface is half-fluid.*

---

* *John Donne: Life, Mind and Art*, John Carey, Faber and Faber, 1981, p192

Poets on poetry

"I think it would be best described as the only possible reaction to a particular kind of experience, a feeling that you are the only one to have noticed something, something especially beautiful or sad or significant. [A poem is] a verbal device that will set off the same experience in other people, so that they too will feel How beautiful, how significant, how sad, and the experience will be preserved, I suppose the kind of response I am seeking from the reader is Yes, I know what you mean, life is like that."
Philip Larkin on why he wrote poetry

"Poetry is a language in which man explores his own amazement."
Christopher Fry

"Genuine poetry can communicate before it is understood."
T.S. Eliot

"A poet's work is to name the unnameable, to point at frauds, to take sides, start arguments, shape the world, and stop it going to sleep."
Salman Rushdie

"Poetry lies its way to the truth."
John Ciardi

W. B. Yeats (1865 – 1939)

"We make out of the quarrel with others, rhetoric, but out of the quarrel with ourselves, poetry."
W.B. Yeats

"A poem is like a shot of expresso – the fastest way to get a way of mental and spiritual energy."
Jeanette Winterson

SECTION

CHAPTER 4

IMAGERY

"Poetry is language at its most distilled and most powerful."
(Rita Dove)

To understand a car, we need to know roughly what goes on under the bonnet. It's the same with poetry. We have considered *what* poems say – their argument, themes, the emotions behind them, the tensions within them. We will now think about *how* they say what they say.

We have already looked how poets use words in striking and unexpected ways. What is any poem, after all, but a string of words arranged into lines? Indeed, a useful exercise if a word surprises you is to ask: how different would the effect be if the poet had used the obvious word instead? It makes you think about the word the poet *does* use – and why it is there. So we noticed, for example, that Thomas Hardy used *wasting* not *wasted* in "I look into my glass" – because *wasting* makes it seem as if the process is happening now, at this very moment.

What poetry often does is anchor big, abstract ideas in concrete language, in a world of things we can see, touch, hear or smell. In the poems we have looked at so far a lot of the language is drawn from nature: roses, holly, worms, daffodils along a bay, starry skies, the badger. Living in towns and cities – as most people do these days – is one of the greatest sources of difficulty for a modern reader. We are cut off from the natural world which most writers in history lived close to, and understood.

So going for a good walk in the country, and keeping your eyes peeled when you do, is probably as good a way of preparing to read literature as anything you'll read in a guide. But in the meantime let's have an under-the-bonnet look at four aspects of poetry: imagery, sound, rhythm and structure.

* * *

There's a phrase in Latin, *ut pictura poesis*, which means "poetry is like a picture". And poetry is certainly full of pictures. Opening the poetry anthology next to me at random a few times, I find these lines:

> So all day long the noise of battle roll'd
> Among the mountains by the winter sea…

(Alfred, Lord Tennyson)

O Nightingale, that on yon bloomy spray
  Warbl'st at eve, when all the woods are still…

(John Milton)

A region desolate and wild.
Black, chafing water: and afloat,
And lonely as a truant child
In a waste wood, a single boat.

(Matthew Arnold)

You bring them in, a trug of thundercloud,
Neglected in long grass and the sulk
Of a wet summer.

(Gillian Clarke)

That's quite a range of pictures, from the mountains by the sea in the first quotation, to the single boat on a lake, to the flowers brought in from outside. One of the most successful exercises I've ever done was to invite a class to copy out a poem and draw pictures from it on the opposite page. It may sound childish, but childish activities can take us to the fundamentals of reading, which we must take care we are not educated out of.

There are two observations I'd like to make about these images. One is that they are very *exact*. Time after time, when we look at poems, we find that the poet wants to give us something precise: not just a sea, but a *winter* sea, not just water but *black, chafing* water.

In Elizabeth Gaskell's novel, *The Cranford Chronicles*, one of the characters, Mr Holcroft, reads Tennyson's poem, 'The Gardener's Daughter'. He realises that what really fires Tennyson's interest is not the gardener's daughter, but the garden. Tennyson describes

> those eyes
> Darker than darkest pansies, and that hair
> More black than ashbuds in the front of March.

The image sends Mr Holbrook out into the garden to check. Is

POETIC LANGUAGE

"Poetry is truth in its Sunday clothes."
(Joseph Roux)

"Poetic language" refers to the kinds of words we might expect to meet in poetry, but not anywhere else:

*The sun's gaudy chariot rode o'er
the shining mead.*

That sort of thing. We meet such language particularly in older poetry before about 1900. A poem was formal, not casual, a sort of dinner party with words. This produces what critics call **heightened** language:

*Ye distant spires, ye antique towers
That crown the watery glade,
Where grateful Science still adores
Her Henry's holy shade ...*
(Thomas Gray, 1716-1771,
'Ode on a Distant Prospect of Eton College')

This is language in evening dress. It's rather out of fashion now, but it was all the rage for Gray and his readers. The poet is doing everything possible to lift us to a lofty, golden world: archaic terms like *ye, antique* (pronounced *ántic*) and *glade*... the personified *Science*... and the long rolling sentence, itself a sign of language behaving in an elegant and sophisticated manner.

Later poets have largely turned away from the poetic (and before it, too: Hardy was deliberately writing against that style). I wonder what Thomas Gray would have made of John Agard, for

example:
Listen Mr Oxford Don

*Me not no Oxford don
me a simple immigrant
from Clapham Common
I didn't graduate
I immigrate*
(John Agard, 1949 -)

Agard is here using colloquial speech patterns from his native Caribbean. In later verses, the speaker says he is wanted for crimes against the English language:

*... muggin' the Queen's English
is the story of my life.*

The poem is making us think about what we regard as proper and correct in language, and how those who speak differently, perhaps because of their background, can feel rejected by the establishment. Agard's poem is carefully organised: notice the rhyme of *don* and *common*, and the yoking together of *graduate* and *immigrate* to make us reflect on how immigrants may be deprived of education and the chances it provides.

Both Gray and Agard are writing about knowledge and education; but while Gray is praising the establishment in the form of Eton's spires, Agard is having some gentle fun with the Oxford don and the Oxford Dictionary. Their poems are like two paths, one polished and shiny and the other a bit rougher; but they both lead somewhere important.

Tennyson right? Are ashbuds in March *really* black? And he discovers to his surprise that yes, they are. Tennyson is right. "And I've lived all my life in the country; more shame for me not to know," he says to himself. It is an example of how accurate poetic imagery can be.

Show don't tell: the old adage. It is what great poets do with economy and power; their relative freedom from the rules of syntax (sentence structure) or grammar, which confine prose writers, means images can bubble up through poetry in all kinds of extraordinary ways.

The second point worth making is that the pictures I came across don't just involve our sight. They involve other senses, too: *the noise of battle* (hearing), *chafing water* (touch). We might even imagine the smell of the *bloomy spray* and the *long grass*. When other senses are involved, we speak of **sensuous imagery**. Some poems are made entirely of pictures. Here's one:

The Makings of Marmalade

unripe oranges in silk-lined sacks
sow-bristle brushes
china jugs of orange-washing water
one big bowl
pith-paring knives, one for each woman
a mountain of sugar, poured slowly
a small Sevillian well
songsheets against the tedium, in parts
pine cones for burning
silver spoons for licking up the lost bits
a seven-gallon pot
a waxed circle, a sellophane circle, elastic
small pieces of toast

(Gillian Allnut, 1949 -)

This is as close to a painting as a poem can get, presenting an array of objects to the mind's eye. I'm not sure you could summarise the argument of this poem: there are no sentences for an argument to be worked out in. But it does awaken thoughts and feelings, as we imagine the women working meticulously and silently in the hot Spanish (Sevillian) sun, singing songs to make the time pass.

It makes me think of all the labour that lies behind the marmalade on our toast. Poets across the ages have somehow transmuted the "sense impressions" of life and packaged them into words, but some are particularly, magically good.

Most of the images in 'The Making of Marmalade' are concrete images, with the poet giving us vivid impressions of *sow-bristle brushes* and *silver spoons for licking up the lost bits*. But when she describes the *mountain of sugar* she doesn't mean there is an actual mountain. She is using what is called **figurative** speech.

A simple test of a phrase if we're not sure is to ask: "Could it be literally true?" If the answer is no, then it's figurative. It's the language of the impossible. Figurative language can involve various figures of speech, of which by far the most important are **metaphors** and **similies**.

A simile makes an explicit comparison; a metaphor is implicit. In practice this means that a simile involves words such as *like* and *as*, while a metaphor by contrast says more directly that something *is* something else. When Wordsworth writes

> I wandered lonely as a cloud

he is using a simile. So is Matthew Arnold when he writes, in the lines quoted earlier:

> ...and afloat,
> And lonely as a truant child,
> In a waste wood, a single boat.

But when Allnut writes about a mountain of sugar she is using a metaphor. Similarly, Sylvia Plath is using a metaphor in her poem, "Blackberrying", when the speaker describes looking up at choughs (crow-like birds)

> in black, cacophonous flocks –
> Bits of burnt paper wheeling in a blown sky...

The comparison here gets its power from the idea that, in the speaker's imagination, the birds *are* wind-blown *Bits of burnt paper*.

Here are some metaphors from the quotes we looked at earlier:

> The noise of battle roll'd

> the sulk of a wet summer

> a trug of thundercloud
> *[a trug is a kind of basket]*

The metaphor is a remarkable device. It brings together in our mind things that would normally be separate – noise and the action of rolling, summer and sulking, a basket and a cloud. Each one is like a little lab experiment, turning two substances into a strange new one. Metaphors are part of normal speech: a storm of applause, a deep thought. The problem is they get over-used and worn out. But a fresh metaphor, in the right hands, can make the world new again.

When we find a metaphor or simile in a poem, we can ask what effect it has. If we were to analyse the metaphor of *the noise of battle roll'd*, for example, we could say it puts across the booming sound of the battle in a dramatic, memorable way: the sound seems like something solid, bouncing and bashing its way like a boulder through the mountains.

There's one further figure of speech we should look at before we

Sylvia Plath at her typewriter. After her death by suicide in 1963, she was the first poet to be posthumously awarded a Pulitzer Prize.

move on, and that is **personification**. This describes an image where something which isn't a person is given human qualities: *the angry storm, the sun peeped over the hilltops*. We've had at least one example in the poems we have looked at: Hardy complains *But Time, to make me grieve / Part steals, lets part abide*, painting old Father Time as a rather sadistic figure.

Telling, original imagery is at the heart of many great poems: it arises from a particular way of seeing. To Burns, love becomes *a red, red rose*, to John Donne, the sun becomes a *saucy pedantic wretch* and, in Donne's 'A Valediction: Forbidding Mourning', a pair of lovers become, in a memorably witty image, a pair of *stiff twin compasses*:

> If they be two, they are two so
>   As stiff twin compasses are two;
> Thy soul, the fix'd foot, makes no show
>   To move, but doth, if the other do.
>
> And though it in the centre sit,
>   Yet, when the other far doth roam,
> It leans, and hearkens after it,
>   And grows erect, as that comes home.

It is the delicacy with which the compasses are imagined which is so remarkable, as John Carey says. It is achieved by the verbs.

> The fixed foot *leanes, and hearkens*, as if bending its ear yearningly to catch some news of its companion. The moving foot *far doth rome* – and the verb makes it sound as if it is travelling trackless wastes, rather than drawing a circle on a sheet of paper... Donne feels with the compasses, and endows them with feeling.*

Stephen Spender's poem, 'An Elementary School Class Room in a Slum', is an effort to open our eyes to poverty and suffering. But it makes its political point far more powerfully for the way in which, rather than preaching, it plunges us into the world of the classroom, where we find:

> Far far from gusty waves these children's faces.
> Like rootless weeds, the hair torn round their pallor: The tall
> girl with her weighed-down head. The paper-
> seeming boy, with rat's eyes. The stunted, unlucky heir
> Of twisted bones, reciting a father's gnarled disease,
> His lesson from his desk. At back of the dim class
> One unnoted, sweet and young. His eyes live in a dream,
> Of squirrel's game, in the tree room, other than this.

The portraits get progressively worse, less recognisably human: a girl with her head weighed down (with unhappiness or disability?); a boy so thin he seems to be made out of paper; a child so poor all that he has to inherit is the *twisted bones* of rickets. But then, at the end of the list, and the back of the class, a ray of hope: a boy, *sweet and young*, whose *eyes live in a dream*, and seem to be inhabiting their own world of imagery, a world *other than this*.

Here we come full circle: if the imagery of Spender's poem sharpens our sense of a world with which we are unfamiliar, one of the inhabitants of that world is shown turning to imagery as a means of escape from it.

---

* Carey, p272

SOUND

"Poetry begins, I dare say," T.S. Eliot once told an audience at Harvard, "with a savage beating a drum in a jungle." Eliot believed that when we first read a great poem it operates on us at a deeper level than words; it doesn't matter if we don't immediately understand it. When Eliot originally read Dante's 'Inferno', he tells us, he read it in the original Italian before he had even learnt the language.

Sound and sense in poetry are always closely linked. In his *Essay on Criticism* (1711), Alexander Pope says: "The sound must seem an echo to the sense." He goes on in the lines that follow to offer some examples of his principle at work:

Soft is the strain when Zephyr* gently blows,
And the smooth stream in smoother numbers flows;
But when loud surges lash the sounding shore,
The hoarse, rough verse should like the torrent roar.

The impression of smoothness is created by the relaxed movement
and expansive repetitions of the second line here – *smoother numbers*
sounds like a lilting repetition of *smooth stream* – just as the jumbling
of *ou*, *ur*, *oar* sounds and bunching of stresses conveys roughness in
the fourth. But what the lines really show is how inseparably sound
and sense in poetry are entangled. As Michael O'Neill comments,
drawing attention to the latitude in Pope's word *seem*:

> The way the words sound will be part of their sense, just as
> in ordinary language use a person's tone of voice does not so
> much echo as establish sense.**

Here is a poem by Tennyson:

The Eagle

He clasps the crag with crooked hands;
Close to the sun in lonely lands,
Ring'd with the azure world, he stands.

The wrinkled sea beneath him crawls;
He watches from his mountain walls,
And like a thunderbolt he falls.

A good way to appreciate the sound of this poem is to take a short
phrase and let it work on us. *He clasps the crag*. On the word *clasps*

---

* The west wind
***Poetic Form: An Introduction* by Michael D. Hurley and Michael O'Neill, CUP, 2012, p6

with its bristling, clicking consonants I can feel the grip this great bird has on its stony perch. And in *crag* the hard sounds capture the hard, jagged rock – a crag is like a *cliff* or *crevasse*. Reading the rest of the line, on *crooked* we feel the talons curling around the rock.

These repeated *c* consonants are **alliteration**. But the word is less important than the effect the sounds have, helping us to imagine, to feel the scene physically. It's worth remembering that Tennyson didn't *have* to use these words; he could have said: *He holds the rock with spreading hands*. But the effect we've just been observing would have been lost. The *what* would be the same, but the *how* would be different, and so our experience would be different.

A FAMOUS MODERN IMAGE

In "The Love Song of J Alfred Prufrock", the modernist poet T. S. Eliot starts by leading us into what promises to be a beautiful image of the evening; but then he twists it, savagely, into an image which has become one of the most famous lines in modern poetry:

Let us go then, you and I,
When the evening is spread out against the sky
Like a patient etherised upon a table...

What's going on here? The first line is metrical; in other words it has an even rhythm. It is quite sing-song, in fact. We might expect a second line to go something like *When the evening spreads the sky*. But our expectations are confounded. Instead, the *lines themselves* spread out. What we get is something like iambic pentameter (see next section), but then in the third line it goes on getting less and less regular. And it's that third line which gives us the weird, puzzling image of a patient under *ether*, meaning anaesthetic. Now, patients under anaesthesia are not a common feature of love songs; nor are they very popular as similes for sunsets. The poem has started in a normal, welcoming way – *Let us go* – and quite soon it has taken us somewhere very strange.

There's more to be said about the *patient* etherised image. For as well as being an anaesthetic, ether has another old sense: it can mean the clear sky, the upper region beyond the clouds, and that obviously works here, too. This is a modern picture, but rooted in the past.

Even after the opening of the poem, we can start thinking about themes. A romantic promise (*Let us go...*) soon leads to this bleak picture of a patient on a table. Critics call this defamiliarisation: take something we're used to, like a sunset, and make it look new and strange. Painters do the same sort of thing. Paintings and poetic images can make us look at the world in a new way.

In the rest of the poem, and in T. S. Eliot's other writings, we find variations of the same thing: the experience of life comes over as complicated, fragmentary, hard to make sense of. In his long poem, "The Waste Land", we get a picture of the soul of modern man as sick, lost in a world which has lost its meaning and its magic. All of this was partly a response to a world which had been ripped to pieces by a world war ("Prufrock" was published in 1917). And all of this vision of man and the world is embedded in the imagery. T.S. Eliot's poetry can be difficult. But then, as he pointed out, modern life, too, can be difficult, so poetry which tries to express modern life is bound to be complex and demanding.

Lord Alfred Tennyson (1809 – 1892)

Another sound effect in these lines is the simple one of **rhyme**. Tennyson uses a triple rhyme, quite unusual in English: *hands*, *lands*, *stands*. What's the effect of this? One thing rhyme does is form a pattern which we find pleasing. Repetition gives a shape to things. And deep down we humans do seem to like shape, repetition, expecting something and then getting it after a little suspense-building wait.

Rhyming speaks to our deep desire for order over disorder, pattern over chaos.

Reading Tennyson's poem, we become alert to the precise sounds and consider how they might relate to what the poem describes. For example, those words that end in *ands* are quite drawn out – a vowel, then an *n* which we can keep going, then moving over the *d* to the soft s: *la... n... ds*. If I think hard of the image and then say 'lands' here I can see a vast plain – *annn* – disappearing into the horizon of *ds*.

"Tennyson might not have meant that, you're reading far too much into it," you might say. But Tennyson thought *a lot* about sounds, and even if he didn't think this exact thought, it is, in a sense, our poem as well as it is his. He wrote it; we're reading it. Reading is itself a creative act – an act of discovery and interpretation, just as a pianist playing a Beethoven piece is making all sorts of interpretive decisions with the music the composer has given him.

To be technical: repetition of consonants is **alliteration**: *round the rough and ragged rocks rude and raucous rascals run*. Repetition of a final syllable (vowel plus consonants) is **rhyme**. Another kind of repetition is to repeat vowels. To spot this, you really have to listen in. But we find it in the lines above: *crag... hands / Close... lonely / sea... beneath*. The repetition of vowel sounds is called **assonance**. The combined effect of alliteration, assonance and rhyme in these lines is to make us much more aware of the sounds of language than we normally are. They make the poetry into a piece of verbal music.

There are a couple of other technicalities to deal with, involving rhyme. The kind of rhyme Tennyson is using is called **full rhyme** – consonant and vowel sounds are repeated. But you'll also find rhymes, especially in modern poetry, which are wafer-thin:

> It seemed that out of battle I escaped
> Down some profound dull tunnel, long since scooped
> Through granites which titanic wars had groined.

Yet also there encumbered sleepers groaned …

(Wilfred Owen, from "Strange Meeting")

In *escaped / scooped* we can see that the poet has hung on to the consonant sounds but sort of twisted the vowel. Owen was a great experimenter with rhyme, and wanted to move away from the rather heavy effect that full final rhyme can create. The rhymes he uses are called **half rhymes** or **slant rhymes**. They are used a lot in modern poetry.

Many poets turned away from full rhymes in the early part of the 20th century. The horror of the First World War played its part in this; somehow the harmony we feel in proper rhyming would have seemed false to the poets caught up in the dreadful day-to-day carnage on the Western Front. Owen's use of half rhymes helps to create a sense of discord in his war poetry, of everything somehow being amiss and out of harmony.

> Happy are men who yet before they are killed
> Can let their veins run cold.
> Whom no compassion fleers
> Or makes their feet
> Sore on the alleys cobbled with their brothers.
> The front line withers.
> But they are troops who fade, not flowers
> For poets' tearful fooling:
> Men, gaps for filling:
> Losses, who might have fought
> Longer; but no one bothers.

The tension in this poem, 'Insensibility', is between feeling and the lack of it; better, the poem suggests, to be callous and indifferent to suffering amidst all this almost unimaginable carnage; better to be insensible, or insensitive, than to give way to strong feeling. "Feeling can kill," as Terry Eagleton puts it: "any too-powerful emotion is likely to make the soldiers more vulnerable" – the soldiers need to behave coldly and callously; if they are emotional they will act in ways which make their terrible situation even worse.

'Insensibility' even "denies its own status as poetry, which in these conditions can be no more than tearful fooling".* Owen could write sensuous and lyrical poetry but here the language is anything but: it is austere, deliberately unpoetic. "The line *The front line withers* stands starkly isolated and end-stopped, four laconic words marooned at the verse's centre," says Eagleton. And the half-rhymes are haunting and uncomfortable: *killed / cold; fleers / flowers; feet / fought; footling / filling: brothers / withers / bothers.*

* * *

Finally, we should consider the term **onomatopoiea**. This is used to describe words where the sounds seem remarkably close to the meaning: *Splash! Squelch!* Maybe *crag* could be called onomatopoiec, bundling up those hard *c* and *g* sounds. If we think we find a close resemblance between sound and sense we can suggest in our reading that there is an onomatopoiec effect. For example, at the end of Tennyson's poem, there's a pause after *thunderbolt*, then *he falls*. Whoosh! Light sounds and a short phrase to evoke the eagle hurtling down from his craggy perch. If you can explain *why* you're seeing or feeling that effect, then you're safe to call it onomatopoeia. And it's good spelling practice, too. It's not every day you write a word which has four vowels in a row.

---

* *How to Read a Poem* by Terry Eagleton, Blackwell 2007, p132-33

CHAPTER 6

RHYTHM

Rhythm finds its way into language early in our lives, from the cooing and singing we heard as babies, to clapping games in the playground, to nursery rhymes: ***Little Miss Muffet sat on a tuffet*** ...

The first thing we need to think about, in considering rhythm, is the beat. And to follow the beat, we need to think about syllables. **Beat** is stress, and in language stress falls on syllables. In any word, there's a syllable that gets extra oomph, which is the **stressed** one.

Rhythm emerges when we organise the beat syllables so they fall into a regular pattern, like objects on a shelf. This is a verse from the master Edward Lear's *Book of Nonsense* (1846):

There was an old person of Fife,
Who was greatly disgusted with life;
They sang him a ballad,
And fed him on salad,
Which cured that old person of Fife.

Now, having contemplated the wisdom in this poem, listen to the beats. If we say it aloud, pushing out the stresses, we get

There **was** an old **per**son of **Fife**,
Who was **great**ly dis**gus**ted with **life**.

The lines both have three stresses, fairly evenly placed. You can clap along to it, in even groups of three. There follow a couple of lines of two stresses (*and **sang** him a **ballad***), then a final one of three, giving a

MASCULINE AND FEMININE RHYMES

The basic rhymes in English are known as *masculine* rhymes. This means they come in the last syllable of the line, as in William Blake's famous poem, 'Tyger Tyger':

When the stars threw down their spears
And water'd heaven with their tears,
Did He smile His work to see?
Did He who made the lamb make thee?

In masculine rhymes it is the last syllable of the line which is stressed (*spears / tears; see / thee*).

So-called *feminine* rhymes are more subtle: they usually occur in words which have more than one syllable, with the second last syllable stressed and containing the rhyme sound: *greeting, retreating; dearly, nearly; master, plaster; Putney; chutney.* Feminine rhymes often showcase a poet's ingenuity: they bring words together in unusual combinations, as when W.H. Auden outlines his preference for a Midlands panorama over a Wordsworthian landscape in "Letter to Lord Byron":

Clearer than Scafell Pike,
my heart has stamped on
The view from Birmingham
to Wolverhampton.

There are times when poets simply enjoy revelling in their rhyming skills. The famously suave Lord Byron himself loved to cut a dash in his poetry, as in these lines, with their mixture of masculine, feminine and, in the last couplet, half rhymes, which he scribbled in the margins of his masterpiece Don Juan.

I would to heaven that I
were so much clay,
As I am blood, bone,

typical limerick formation of 3-3-2-2-3. And to add to the pattern, the three-stress lines are bound together by rhyme sound, and the middle two by another rhyme: *aabba*.

Here's the start of a poem by the Cornish writer Charles Causley:

Timothy Winters

Timothy Winters comes to school
With eyes as wide as a football-pool,
Ears like bombs and teeth like splinters:
A blitz of a boy is Timothy Winters.

***Timothy Winters** comes to school* ... four strong beats you can clap along to. And you can keep the clapping going through the next three lines, and the rest of the poem, too.

---

        marrow, passion, feeling –
Because at least the past
        were passed away –
And for the future – (but I
        write this reeling,
Having got drunk
        exceedingly today,
So that I seem to stand
        upon the ceiling)
I say – the future is
        a serious matter –
And so – for God's sake –
        hock and soda water!

The poem is a cry to live in the moment, free from the consciousness of past and future. Its energy seems to fulfil that wish. There's clearly a very intricate rhyming structure at work here (a-b-a-b-a-b-c-c); at the same time the rhymes themselves often seem to fall into place just by chance. And the end of the stanza has a slightly tipsy feel to it, with its cry for *wine and water* undercutting the solemn claim that *the future is a serious matter*.

Look at the chain of rhymes that flows from *feeling*. The word is given prominence at the head of a list of earthly things Byron wants to rid himself of. It is not an easy word to rhyme on, but for Byron this difficulty becomes an opportunity to show his skill: the word *reeling* puts the skids under any temptation in us to believe too much in his *feeling* – and offers an apt description of what the verse does as it wheels from line to line; the next rhyme, on *ceiling*, is even bolder; it overturns any sense we may have of lingering sincerity. Byron is having fun. The stanza is a party of sounds and wit.

William Wordsworth (1770 – 1850)

Notice, by the way, how Causley is using many of the other poetic devices we have looked at: rhyme (the lines here rhyme in pairs, so are called **rhyming couplets**), alliteration (*blitz of a boy*), simile (one each for eyes, ears, teeth), metaphor (*A blitz of a boy*). All of these are working with the rhythm to put into our minds a big, dishevelled, powerful boy.

Now let's look at, or rather listen to, some famous lines by Shakespeare:

> Shall **I** com**pare** thee **to a summ**er's **day?**
> Thou **art** more **lovely and** more **temper**ate.
> Rough **winds** do **shake** the **darl**ing **buds** of **May,**
> And **summ**er's **lease** hath **all** too **short** a **date.**

As before, we find the same number of beats in each line, evenly spread. There were three in the limerick, four in "Timothy Winters", but here we have gone up to five (usually the maximum in an English verse line, though there are some exceptions). And once again the lines are tied together by rhyme as well as rhythm; the rhyme here is in an *abab* pattern.

But you might sense some difference, too. The beats are not quite as "pushed out" as they are in the Causley poem. You might even query the stress I have put on little words like *to* and *and* in the first two lines. And you'd be right. When there are five stresses, one is often weaker than the others. Also, just labelling syllables as stressed and unstressed simplifies matters: there are *grades* of stress. If you say *Rough winds* you might find there's only a slight extra stress on *winds*, and the same with *too short*. So although there is a rhythmic frame, it isn't as obvious as in Causley's poem. It's a little like listening to classical music instead of pop. The beat is there, but it's not as clear.

The beat Shakespeare is writing to in his sonnets is a template of di-DUM, sometimes obviously, sometimes not so obviously, and sometimes taking a little break from it. The technical term for this arrangement of beats is **metre**.

Shakespeare, we noted, is writing to a template of di-DUM. He is using what is called an **iambic pentameter**: an **iamb** is a bundle of two syllables, the first unstressed, the second stressed: di-DUM, to-DAY. And pentameter is just an old word for five (as in pentangle, or pentathlete).

> to**day** to**day** to**day** to**day** to**day**.
> Rough **winds** do **shake** the **dar**ling **buds** of **May**

Now say "morning". You have just uttered a **trochee**: DUM-di, *morning*. Say it four times, and you have come up with a **trochaic tetrameter**, four trochees. Trochee stands for the pair of syllables, tetrameter means four times. An iamb and a trochee are two kinds of metrical **foot**, the technical word for the two syllables bundled together. So we now have five technical terms:

> **Iamb**: an unstressed syllable, then a stressed one: *today, do shake, Peru*
> **Trochee**: stressed-unstressed: *morning, wonder*
> **Tetrameter**: x 4
> **Pentameter**: x 5
> **Foot**: a repeated rhythmic pattern like an iamb or trochee

Here are some lines from a 17th-century poem on the sad subject of a fawn being killed:

The Nymph Complaining for the Death of Her Faun

> The wanton troopers riding by
> Have shot my fawn, and it will die.
> Ungentle men! They cannot thrive –

To kill thee! Thou ne'er didst alive
Them any harm …

(Andrew Marvell, 1621-1678)

As ever, read for the meaning first: the nymph (forest girl) tells us that some men have shot her fawn, then speaks, lamentingly, to the fawn itself: *To kill thee!* (meaning *How could they*). In what way is the poet organising the beats here? There's a fairly clear di-DUM rhythm, and four beats in a line, which makes it, technically, an iambic tetrameter:

The **wan**ton **troo**pers **ri**ding **by**.

What's more notable, though, is where the poet departs from that, at the end:

To **kill** thee! **Thou** ne'er **didst** a**live**
Them any **harm** …

The first line of this is regular, but the exclamation mark suggests a big pause (you can hear the nymph sobbing here). This pause is called a **caesura**. But the real shock to the metrical system comes in the next line. Instead of di-DUM we get a big stress: ***Them…*** DUM! And of course that's what we would say: *You never did **them** any harm!* That variation, stressing *Them*, brings out the emotion of the moment. We were led to expect an iamb and we got a trochee. This variation – which is the most common in English metrical poetry – is called a **trochaic inversion**. And it's the regularity leading up to the variation which gives it its power.

Rhythm is infinitely flexible. Long vowels and stressed syllables slow down the march of words:

> I **look** into my **glass**
> And **view** my **wasting skin**

is made of iambs, but as well as that, in those drawn-out syllables –
glass… view… waste… – with long vowels and prolonged consonants,
we hear the weary, yearning voice of the speaker. It's iambic rhythm
in first gear, the gear for slow viewing, pausing, meditating. Stress and
speech sounds work together.

A knowledge of the technical terms we have been using is not essential
to enjoying, understanding or indeed writing poetry – far from it. The
terms are helpful only in the light they shed on the poet's craft.

* * *

Stevie Smith (1902 – 1971)

The impact of rhythm is most obvious when a poem's lines vary in length. John Betjeman's "I. M. Walter Ramsden", for example, begins with two lines that are dramatically different:

> Dr Ramsden cannot read The Times obituary to-day
> He's dead.

The first line plods on and on, recording what seems an unremarkable observation; the second line gives us a shock. There is something jaunty about the suddenness of the transition from one very long to one very short line, and the sense of comic imbalance is obviously a risk in a poem about someone's death.

But the abruptness of the second line, after the wandering ordinariness of the first, is what makes it so potent: death *does* intrude abruptly.

Stevie Smith controls the rhythm beautifully but disquietingly in her little masterpiece, "Not Waving But Drowning".

> Nobody heard him, the dead man,
> But still he lay moaning:
> I was much further out than you thought
> And not waving but drowning.

> Poor chap, he always loved larking
> And now he's dead.
> It must have been too cold for him his heart gave way,
> They said.

> Oh, no no no, it was too cold always
> (Still the dead one lay moaning)
> I was much too far out all my life
> And not waving but drowning.

The first stanza alternates lines of three stresses with lines of two:

> Nobody **heard** him, the **dead** man,
> But **still** he lay **moan**ing*

The second stanza begins in the same way – a line of three stresses followed by a line of two. The way the shorter lines follow the longer ones heightens the sense of anti-climax around which the poem is built: the mistaking of a desperate gesture for a merely trivial one; it's as if the mistake is easy to make, a sense enhanced by the balancing of the two words in the last line of the first stanza, so that we're forced to see how alike they are, and then by the jaunty

> Poor chap, he always loved larking

followed by the monosyllabic, coldly matter-of-fact

> And now he's dead.

In their rhythm, these two lines echo the first two lines of the first stanza, but then the rhythm goes awry. Instead of two balanced lines

> It must have been too cold for him
> His heart gave way, they said.

we have this:

> It must have been too cold for him his heart gave way
> They said

---

* This uses a kind of foot we haven't yet come across: the *dactyl*. This goes DUM-di-di: *No*body *heard* him, the *dead* man…See p69

The first long, clumsy, unpunctuated line conveys the breathless, confused reaction of the dead man's companions in a way that is all the more powerful because of its disruptive effect on the poem's rhythm. There is a brilliant economy in how these three stanzas convey the tragedy. Smith uses three different tightly woven viewpoints, the poem's rhythm binding them together as she switches between a narrator, the voice of the dead man's companions, and the dead man himself, whose voice returns in the last stanza with the insistent

Oh, no no no, it was too cold always

The tone of sharp rebuke – the procession of monsyllablic words (eight in a row, five of two letters, two of three letters), the three *no*s, the repeated o sounds, the final definitive *always* – drives home to us that the poem is about more than a futile gesture being misinterpreted: the dead man was always an outsider; he was never at home in the world; his larking about was just a pretence:

I was much too far out all my life
And not waving but drowning.

Poetry means more than prose, and few poems concentrate meaning more than this one. Poems mean more because they can express so much in so few words. A poem like this is like a little room. In little rooms every picture, every piece of furniture, every ornament, has to be placed in exactly the right spot. 'Not Waving But Drowning' is very short, miming its subject matter in a small, feeble gesture of protest. It is as if this tiny poem is itself waving out of the white space which surrounds it – waving into a great sea of silence.

STRUCTURE

If we look back at the Hardy poem, we'll see that the verses all have a third line which is a bit longer than the others:

> I look into my glass
> And view my wasting skin,
> And say, 'Would God it came to pass
> My heart had shrunk as thin.'

And we notice, too, that the lines are tied together with rhyme. Hardy here is using a shape that comes up time and again in verse and songs: a first line, then a second line repeating or developing its idea, then a third line that reaches out like a hand in the dark, then a fourth that comes back and settles the verse to a close. "Happy birthday" has that shape, and so do hundreds of hymns. Bob Dylan's "Shelter from the Storm" follows exactly that pattern, verse after hypnotising verse. And so do countless other four-line verses. This shape, for statements in verse and song, is as familiar as a vase for flowers. And it affects the meaning: each verse or **stanza** is a statement, a reaching out, and a settling back. Without telling us, the speaker is composing his feelings as he is uttering them. Hardy's poem is not just about growing old, but feeling passions; it is about how we manage and contain the passions that rush through us. It is beautifully controlled and organised.

We humans are order-making creatures, leading, for the most part, structured existences. Our houses are divided into rooms, which are separated by walls. The sofa I'm looking at has two cushions, roughly equidistant. Poetry expresses the same need for arrangement. It is an ordering activity, giving shape to thoughts, feelings and arguments; and the shape is part of the meaning.

Poems find their shape in **lines** and **stanzas**. The following is a complete poem:

Parting at Morning

Round the cape of a sudden came the sea,
And the sun looked over the mountain's rim:
And straight was the path of gold for him*
And the need of a world of men for me.

(Robert Browning, 1812-1889)

What can we say about how this poem is organised? Without even reading a word, we can confidently state that it is in four lines, in one

---

* *'him'* refers to the sun

group or stanza. In this case, it is a four-line verse called a **quatrain**. And the lines are grouped in a clear rhyme scheme of *abba*. Listening for the rhythm, we can hear four strong beats in each line, so we can say that the poem is organised into quite a regular metre (with slight variations, an iambic tetrameter).

There are other features worth noting. Each line contains a single **clause**; that is to say you could get out of each one a grammatical sentence that would make sense on its own. Lines 1 and 2 end with punctuation, marking off the clause. They are what we call **end-stopped**: lines 2, 3 and 4 all start with *And*.

We have identified the structure of the poem by line, stanza, metre, rhyme, and sentence; and we have noticed the little feature of **repetition** with that *And*. The next step is to link these observations to the meaning and effect. Reading the poem again, we find that it records a particular moment – the sea and the sun appearing to the speaker, presumably as he walks along. The last line is not easy, but it tells us that while the sun will trace his daily course, his *path of gold*, the speaker needs to return (from what?) to *the world of men*.

If there is a central tension here, it is between the rapture of the solitary speaker and his desire for the company of other humans. He cannot share the golden world of the sun. Perhaps the title, 'Parting at Morning', gives us a clue, suggesting that he is parting from a beloved. It is possible, though less likely, that he is parting from his dentist. But in either case this moment of revelation is what the poem records: the sight of the sun and sea in their splendour, followed by the speaker's reflection that he needs to get back to society.

The poem takes this experience, which must have happened in a flash, and structures it clearly so that we can follow it as a story: the sea appears (line 1), then the sun (2), then we think about the sun's path (3), then the man's path (4). Each line traces out a complete thought, chained by *And* to the next.

The structure gives a shape and a sense to the passing joy and impulse.

And this shape makes it accessible to us: a scattering of sensations and feelings is turned into a calm series of statements. It builds up expectations – we wait for the rhyme sound to *sea* to appear, and we wait for the chain of statements to conclude in a full stop. The end of the poem resolves these expectations, bringing the reading to a satisfying close. Like Wordsworth remembering the daffodils, Browning remembers this moment in the morning and, in remembering, sorts it out into an ordered scheme. And with this ordering, the experience becomes visible and comprehensible to us.

Without this frame, the meaning and the feeling would vanish. Poems, like houses, need to be well built if they are to last.

* * *

Poets divide their work into verses, or stanzas, in very different ways and to all kinds of different effect; often we may hesitate between one verse and the next; sometimes the poet hurries us on across the break; sometimes the divisions seem random, at other times highly regular.

Hardy's 'The Voice' – one of the great poems he wrote after the death of his first wife, Emma – uses stanzas to great effect. He had become estranged from Emma before she died; they continued to live in the same house, but apart. Her death in 1912, however, provoked Hardy to write a whole series of intensely felt poems of remorse and guilt but also of extraordinary recollection of their time together.

We don't need to know any of this to understand 'The Voice'. In its raw intensity of feeling it is both highly personal and yet transcends the personal:

> Woman much missed, how you call to me, call to me,
> Saying that now you are not as you were

Thomas Hardy (1840 – 1928)

When you had changed from the one who was all to me,
But as at first, when our day was fair.

Can it be you that I hear? Let me view you, then,
Standing as when I drew near to the town
Where you would wait for me: yes, as I knew you then,
Even to the original air-blue gown!

Or is it only the breeze, in its listlessness
Travelling across the wet mead to me here,
You being ever dissolved to wan wistlessness,
Heard no more again far or near?

Thus I; faltering forward,
Leaves around me falling,
Wind oozing thin through the thorn from norward,
And the woman calling.

The poem begins with an insistent rhythm, or metre, and it's an unusual one in English poetry – DUM-di-di DUM-di-di – classically known as a **dactyl** (dacty (*l*) comes from the Greek word for finger: one long bone, then two short ones, hence one stressed syllable followed by two unstressed ones). That rhythm persists through the poem as Hardy recollects his meetings with Emma, wondering whether what he's hearing in the breeze is her voice, while all the time knowing, of course, that it isn't her voice. He is just imagining it.

The first line of the poem is direct and clear, but quite soft – *Woman much missed, how you call to me, call to me* – with the alliteration of the two *m*s in *much missed*, and the echo in *call to me, call to me*. The sentence then unwinds in a confused, faltering way, the short words piling up as Hardy struggles to understand his confused feelings. The tortured syntax suggests a mind in turmoil, as tortured syntax often does:

> Saying that now you are not as you were
> When you had changed from the one who was all to me

The second stanza is smoother, more balanced as Hardy recalls a happier time, ending with the precise and lovely image of the *original air-blue gown*:

> Standing as when I drew near to the town
> Where you would wait for me: yes, as I knew you then,
> Even to the original air-blue gown!

In the third stanza the mood shifts again, as Hardy realises he is deceiving himself: the listless breeze blowing across the *wet* mead contrasts with the *fair* day of the second stanza. The woman's image *dissolves into wan wistlessness*, a haunting phrase which no one but Hardy could have thought of: wistlessness is a word which doesn't exist. Hardy has invented it, evoking wistfulness as in yearning regret and repeating, in a discomfiting rhyme, the idea of listlessness. (When a writer invents a word, it is known as a **neologism**.)

But the stroke of genius in Hardy's poem, as the Oxford professor of poetry, Seamus Perry says, comes in the fourth stanza. Until this point the rhythm has varied only a little; now Hardy breaks the pattern altogether and we have in the rhythm and metre of the last stanza a brilliant enactment of his own faltering.

> Thus I; faltering forward,
> Leaves around me falling,
> Wind oozing thin through the thorn from norward,
> And the woman calling.

In metrical terms, says Perry, it is hard to know how to scan this last line. It seems to float free from the poem into a piece of human speech, giving it an extraordinary power. The metrical/rhythmical expectations of the first three verses are gracefully established. Then suddenly the poem falls to pieces in a beautiful, artful way, which mirrors the poet's own state of mind, since this is a poem about Hardy himself falling to pieces. His faltering is communicated not only in the meaning of the words but, brilliantly, in its rhythm too.*

* * *

All sorts of things combine to give 'The Voice' its power. One of them is its structure: one by one the stanzas lead the reader through the poet's changing mood to the breakdown at the end.

The structure, or architecture, of poetry can be very subtle, an effect we hardly notice as we read through a poem, and often it is deliberately low key. Sometimes though it is the opposite, with poems divided into regular stanzas which match a regular rhythm.

Occasionally, the structural effect of verses can be visual too. The poet-priest George Herbert (1593-1633) used every means at his disposal to expound Christian doctrine.

Here, simple words and a simple shape combine to make sure we know the meaning of the altar in Herbert's Anglican Christian teaching. As we follow the ideas of penitence and sacrifice, so we match it with an image of an altar in our mind, and see one – the base – the stand – the tabletop – on the page before us:

---

* The discussion of 'The Voice' owes much to Seamus Perry: you can see him talking to Jolyon Connell about this poem on YouTube

The Altar

A broken Altar, Lord, thy servant reares,
Made of a heart, and cemented with teares:
   Whose parts are as thy hand did frame;
    No workmans tool hath touched the same
        A Heart alone
        Is such a stone
        As nothing but
        Thy pow'r doth cut.
        Wherefore each part
        Of my hard heart
        Meets in this frame,
        To praise thy name.
   That if I chance to hold my peace,
   These stones to praise thee may not cease.
O let thy blessed SACRIFICE be mine,
And sanctifie this ALTAR to be thine.

Another example of concrete poetry is Alice Oswald's poem, *Dart*, published in 2002. This is written in so-called *free verse*: it has no regular metre or rhyme. The poem traces the River Dart in Devon from source to mouth, and part of its effect is physical: its shape reflecting the contours of the river itself. In the upper reaches it encounters a walker as it flows long:

> What I love is one foot in front of another. South-south-west and down the contours. I go slipping between Black Ridge and White Horse Hill into a bowl of the moor where echoes can't get out
>
> listen,

a
lark
spinning
around
one
note
splitting
and
mending
it

and I find you in the reeds, a trickle coming out of a bank, a
foal of a river

one step-width water
of linked stones
trills in the stones
glides in the trills
eels in the glides
in each eel a fingerwidth of sea

The impact of all this is as much physical as intellectual. It affects us as
much through its shape and movement as through what is said: from the
prose which enacts the *one foot in front of another* progress of the walker,
to the sudden shot of lyricism that sends a sentence spinning one word
at a time over the line breaks like the note that the lark *splits and mends*,
back to another trickle of prose as the walker's monologue tries to start
up again, before the poem gets diverted back to the course of the river
once more, picking up momentum like the verse itself as it finds a form
in which words start to cascade from one short line to the next. The
rhythm and sound and sense all work together with the visual effect.
They combine to mime the experience the poet is talking about.

CHAPTER 8

LINE ENDINGS

Poets use all sorts of tricks and techniques, and volumes have been devoted to the intricacies of structure, rhythm, rhyme, metre, sound and imagery. We need to remember, however, that these techniques only matter because of the effect they have; in their different ways they all contribute to the surprise, tension or conflict we find in poems, and reinforce the sentiments poets are seeking to express.

Take the way poets use lines – in particular how they *end* lines. Here is Chaucer describing the Cook in his General Prologue to *The Canterbury Tales*:

He coude rost, and seeth*, and broil, and frye,

boil

Maken mortreaux,* and well bake a pie.

stew

But greet harm was it, as it thoughte me,
That on his shin a mormal* hadde he.

open sore

For a blankmanger,* that made he with the best.

blancmange

When lines correspond with grammatically complete units like this they are described as **end-stopped**. And usually, as here, end-stopped lines will end with some form of punctuation: a comma, a semi-colon, a full stop.

Chaucer's little pictures, or vignettes, of his various pilgrims in the General Prologue often use a succession of end-stopped lines to list details about them in a rapid-fire way. He enjoys the possibilities they afford for jumbling up all kinds of often wildly different qualities or attributes: the cook's blancmange sounds distinctly less appetising once we've been told about the open sore on his shin, but the diverse characteristics are all thrown in as part of the mix.

Sometimes, endstopping can support an effort to impose order, as in these thoughts on a rejected suitor written by Elizabeth I:

I grieve and dare not show my discontent,
I love and yet am forced to seem to hate,
I do, yet dare not say I ever meant,
I am stark mute but inwardly do prate.
I am and am not, I freeze and yet am burned,
Since from myself another self I turned.

The Queen's emotions may be muddled, but in the verse she tries, literally, to get her feelings into line, neatly fulfilling a much later definition W. H. Auden gave of poetry as "the clear expression of mixed feelings".

See how each line holds two contradictory emotions alongside one another – grief and composure, love and hate, silence and inward torment – before the passage reaches a climax as *two* conflicting impulses are crowded together in its second last line. The verse, then, clarifies the Queen's feelings: whether writing it helped her to triumph over her turmoils or just made them worse is open to question.

End-stopping emphasises the integrity of the individual line. An end-stopped line can even seem to take on a life of its own, part of the poem it belongs to yet also somehow separate from it.

> What will survive of us is love.

This famous line by Philip Larkin comes at the end of 'An Arundel Tomb', a poem which seems to say almost exactly the opposite. It is as if the single-sentence last line somehow breaks free or is sealed off from the gloomy picture which comes before it; it encloses a hope, a hope the poet knows is not justified but defiantly not only includes but, because it is a final thought, makes the most important in his poem.

Now let us return to a poem we looked at earlier:

The Sick Rose

O Rose thou art sick.
The invisible worm
That flies by night
In the howling storm:

Has found out thy bed
Of secret joy:

And his dark secret love
Does thy life destroy.

This poem is in eight lines, grouped in two quatrains. Like the poem by Browning we looked at earlier, it is bound together by metre, with two strong beats in the line, falling on two key words: *O **Rose** thou art **sick**.* There is rhyme, but only in the second and fourth lines.

There are two main differences between Blake's poem and Browning's: first, Blake's lines are short; secondly, they do not correspond with clauses (a clause is a statement that could stand as a sentence on its own). Lines two and three are not end-stopped, nor are lines five and seven; and the punctuation is odd. The colon at the end of the first verse breaks up the sentence and seems to be there to make us pause for a moment. It comes a surprise to realise that the whole poem is made up of just two sentences.

So why set it out like this? One answer is that the short lines focus our attention: *the invisible worm* stands out because it is given a whole line to itself. This is a poem we are clearly intended to read phrase by phrase, taking our time over each one. Another effect is that the short, two-stress lines form a pattern we expect, so when it is broken and we get *three* stressed key words in *dark secret love* there is a real drama to it: here, we sense, is where the core of the poem lies.

After the first line, the lines also run into each other as the sentence unwinds. This is a device called **enjambment**, French for "striding". We can say that *the invisible worm / that flies by night* is an instance of enjambment, but we are not saying anything interesting until we suggest what the *effect* of that is. Here, I suggest, there is a kind of double motion: we pause on *worm* because it is the end of the line, and a key and intriguing word, but we also feel the need to read on from it to make sense. The enjambment places emphasis on the line ending. It also creates a sense of suspense: we pause on an image before it develops into something bigger.

William Blake's Ancient of Days *(1794). Blake accompanied many of his poems with engravings, often involving religious imagery.*

It is usually the case that the more sentences move across line endings, the greater the effect of turbulence, of the mind making an effort to arrange thoughts, sensations and feelings. It's interesting that while Browning is writing about his experience in the past tense, Blake is in the present. The moment of finding the sick rose is happening *now*: the poem is a record of the effort to capture this vision as it occurs to him.

Sometimes poets use enjambments to surprise us, as in these lines by Wordsworth's near-contemporary, Thomas Lovell Beddoes, spoken by a character in his play *Death's Jest-Book*:

> I could not wish him in my rage to die
> Sooner...

The first line tricks us. The poet is saying: *However furious I am, I wouldn't want him to die*. We think Beddowes is about to add something generous. But he doesn't: lurking round the corner of the line is the word 'Sooner', which creates a last-minute twist of the knife. He is saying not that he *doesn't* want the man to die but that he *does* (though not too soon).

Here are the first few lines of a famous poem by W.H. Auden called 'Musée des Beaux Arts':

> About suffering they were never wrong,
> The Old Masters; how well they understood
> Its human position; how it takes place
> While someone else is eating or opening a window
>   or just walking dully along...

Auden is telling us how the great painters of the past, the Old Masters, understood the truth about human suffering – how it is very intense, making us feel we should take it seriously, yet happens while most of us are busily getting on with our everyday lives and paying no attention. That is the central conflict of the poem.

The tone is casual and chatty. Look at the way the poem starts. The obvious way of starting would have been:

> The Old Masters were never wrong about suffering.

But Auden instead changes the natural word order, or syntax, and *reverses* the two phrases, making his opening line much more interesting and giving emphasis to the crucial word *suffering*, with its three heavy syllables, by placing it so early.

> About suffering, they were never wrong

And just as Blake makes us wait after the word *worm*, Auden then adds a small, extra sense of drama by making us wait to know who *they* are – the people who were never wrong. We have a moment of suspense at the end of the line before we learn the truth.

> About suffering, they were never wrong,
> The Old Masters…

It's a classic example of the use of enjambment. As the critic Terry Eagleton has put it, we have "to step across the line-ending to find out exactly who was never wrong about suffering". And the poem's "air of well-bred worldliness" – as if we're hearing from someone who's seen a lot and is quietly giving us his reflections on life – is kept up by the constant use of enjambments and the mixture of short lines and long ones. So suffering, we're told, takes place

> While someone else is eating or opening a window
> or just walking dully along…

W. H. Auden (1907 - 1973)

This is a stumbling, untidy line; there seem to be too many words in it; the poet is perhaps suggesting that the line is a bit like life itself – all those experiences we have piling up, one on top of the other, while elsewhere there is suffering going on which, most of the time, we're not aware of. That, so the poet seems to say, is just the way things are. Although the Auden poem is less formal in its structure than either Blake's or Browning's, it is carefully designed – though in a way which makes us think it isn't. It even rhymes, very discreetly (*wrong / along*), with the enjambments, making it hard to spot the rhymes as the thoughts flow freely on from one line to the next.

Many modern poems are much less formal even than Auden's 'Musée des Beaux Arts'. Take this one by Moniza Alvi:

Exile

The old land swinging in her stomach
she must get to know this language
better - key words, sound patterns
wordgroups of fire and blood.

Try your classmates with
the English version of your name.
Maria. Try it.
Good afternoon. How are you?

I am fine. Your country -
you see it in a drop of water.
The last lesson they taught you there
was how to use a gun.

And now in stops and starts
you grow a second city in your head.

It is Christmas in this school.
Sarajevo is falling through

a forest of lit-up trees,
cards and decorations.
Mountains split with gunfire
swallow clouds, birds, sky.

Here we can tell at a glance that the poem is organised into quatrains. The line lengths, though roughly equal, vary. There is no regular rhyme scheme and no regular metre to establish where lines should begin and end.

Enjambments can create little pauses and surprises which would be lost in prose.

Try your classmate with
The English version of your name.

Could this be a teacher speaking? Is the little suspenseful pause after *with* capturing the teacher thinking for a second of a challenge to give the girl? Endings and spaces can suggest the pauses and movements we might make if we were performing the poem to an audience. Later in the poem there is an enjambment between stanzas: *Sarajevo is falling through // a forest of lit-up trees*. Here, the gap on the page between the stanzas seems to suggest the stream of memory, and helps us to realise, I think, that the girl is seeing two things at the same time: the terrible destruction of her home city, and the decorated Christmas tree in front of her. The *lit-up trees* are her childish description of the Christmas trees, but they also bring to mind the image of explosions and gunfire. We wouldn't catch that double image if we weren't pausing for balance on each stepping stone of the poem.

We can only speculate. Of course it is possible that we will see things the poet did not intend, but a possible answer to that thought, as we have noted, is that the writer and the reader *collaborate* in a poem.

* * *

We have now considered *what* poems are saying, and *how* they say them. In English Literature studies, the kind of careful reading we have been attempting is called Practical Criticism. In its purest form, Practical Criticism goes no further than this: we make what we can of the words on the page, without referring to history books or biographies or any other background material. It is like looking at a picture in an art gallery with no idea of where it came from or even who painted it. And we can enjoy most poems, and most poetry, without knowing anything at all about their creator.

All the same, it's not just interesting but helpful to know something about the poets we read. The knowledge can help us make connections between poetry and the world from which it emerges.

Poets in the 14th century, to take an obvious example, wrote very different poetry to the poets of today. This isn't just a matter of the language changing. They had other things on their mind, such as the Black Death, the huge power of the Church, the Last Judgement, and the best route to Canterbury. Their poetry belongs in that world, which we call its **context**.

As to *why* poets write poetry – well, sometimes they tell us what they are trying to do, as when Milton ambitiously sets out in *Paradise Lost* to "justify the ways of God to man", or Wilfred Owen tells us he feels a duty to pass on the reality of what it was like to fight on the Western Front: "all a poet can do today is warn". At other times, we can shrewdly guess that a poem is meant to persuade us to think or feel something. Or we simply take a poem as an invitation to look at things in a new way, to widen our vision of the world. But whatever our approach, we go on listening to the ghosts – and enjoying and contemplating the messages they send us.

Wilfred Owen (1893 - 1918)

A SHORT HISTORY OF ENGLISH VERSE

Old English (700 – 1100)

English starts with the arrival of the Angles and Saxons in the fifth century AD, following the departure of the Romans. Their Germanic languages merged to form Anglo-Saxon, aka Old English, and the earliest writing in it dates from about 700. Old English looks like a foreign language today. The most famous Old English poem is *Beowulf*, a heroic epic with monsters and dragons set in the old Germanic lands. Seamus Heaney's recent translation is a great read.

Middle English (1100 – 1500)

In 1066, the Normans invaded and occupied England. With them came a stock of French words, which mingled with Old English and gradually transformed the language.

Middle English is easier to read than Old English, and the later 14th century is a particularly rich period, with Chaucer's *Troilus and Criseyde* and *The Canterbury Tales* giving us a lively portrait of the medieval world. In the same period William Langland wrote an extraordinary portrait of contemporary life, *Piers Plowman* – passionate, visionary, and angry. And the anonymous "Gawain poet" wrote *Gawain and the Green Knight* and *Pearl*, both of which can be read in brilliant translations by Simon Armitage.

Early Modern (1500 – 1700)

This period includes the Renaissance, when new ideas from the continent, and new learning derived from the study of the classics, poured into English culture.

In the mid-1500s the sonnet appears in its English form; its early practitioners included Edmund Spenser, Sir Philip Sidney and William Shakespeare. (Spenser also wrote the vast *Faerie Queene* (1590-96) which describes the adventures of Arthur's knights, all in an elaborate praise of Queen Elizabeth I, who paid Spenser a £50 pension for his pains, although there is no evidence she ever read it.)

The Renaissance, though, is most famous for its dramatic verse: it was the time of Marlowe (*Dr Faustus*) and Ben Jonson (*The Alchemist*) as well, of course, as Shakespeare who wrote not just his plays but also two long narrative poems, 'Venus and Adonis' and 'The Rape of Lucrece'. The early 1600s, saw the emergence of the so-called "Metaphysical" poets – in particular John Donne, George Herbert and

Andrew Marvell, who wrote poems which are passionate, clever and formally ingenious.

The English Renaissance is often thought to end with John Milton's mighty epic in blank verse, *Paradise Lost* (first version, 1667) – telling the story of Adam and Eve's expulsion from the Garden of Eden – and with his near-contemporary John Dryden, whose 'Annus Mirabilis' (1667) combines narrative, description, inventive imagery and controlled form.

Restoration poetry at the end of the 17th century – following the end of Cromwell's Republic and the restoration to the throne of Charles 11 – is marked by a reaction against the puritanism of writers like Milton and a relish for the pleasures of the good life, particularly love and sex. The Earl of Rochester is perhaps the best known, and certainly the most notorious, of these Cavalier courtly poets.

The 18th century

A good deal of 18th-century poetry is poised, and witty, making sharp observations of the world. This is especially true of Alexander Pope, England's greatest satirical poet, who loved rhyming couplets and is most famous for *The Rape of the Lock*. Other well-known 18th-century poems include Thomas Gray's 'Elegy, Written in a Country Churchyard' and Samuel Johnson's 'The Vanity of Human Wishes'.

The late 18th century sees the dawn of the Romantic movement, with its greater emphasis on personal feeling: the Scottish poet Robert Burns published a selection of his lyrics, The Kilmarnock Volume, in 1786. William Blake's *Songs of Innocence and Experience* (1789-94) deals with the passage of human life and at the same time attacks social injustices of the time.

Alexander Pope (1688 – 1744)

Early 19th century: The Romantics

The English Romantics were above all concerned with celebrating nature and the human imagination. The French Revolution of 1789, with its overthrowing of the old order, was a hugely important moment for the Romantics. The "first generation" Romantics were William Wordsworth and Samuel Taylor Coleridge, who, in their introduction to *Lyrical Ballads*, declared their aim of stripping poetry of ornament and returning it to the language and subjects of ordinary life.

The second generation romantics were Byron, Keats and Shelley. Byron wrote intense lyrics but also satirical and narrative verse. Shelley and Keats composed intense and passionate lyric poetry about human feeling and imagination. All three died tragically young. Somewhat apart from the Romantics is the poet John Clare, whose work brings to vivid life the countryside and its people and customs.

Later 19th century: The Victorians

Following the Romantics came a period of great stylistic variety, under the reign of Queen Victoria (1837-1901). The huge output of Alfred, Lord Tennyson ranges from long narrative poems to short lyrics. His long poem *In Memoriam*, written for a dead friend, is a notable elegy, full of the thoughts that haunted the Victorian mind. Robert Browning developed the dramatic monologue in *Men and Women*. Female poets such as Emily Brontë and Christina Rossetti developed their own styles and forms. The 19th century was also a great age for nonsense verse, in the hands of Lewis Carroll and Edward Lear.

The 20th century

Among the greatest poets of the early 20th century is Thomas Hardy, who considered himself more a poet than a novelist. His lyric poems are notable for their range of form and their depth of feeling, none more so than the poems he wrote remembering his first wife Emma. This period also saw the poets of the First World War of 1914-18: Wilfred Owen and Siegfried Sassoon are the best known. Edward Thomas, who also served, and died, in the war, was prompted to write poetry by his friend the American poet Robert Frost: his work, composed in a short period, presents an intense contemplation of England and the English countryside. Another great poet of the early 20th century is W. B. Yeats, the first Irishman to win the Nobel Prize for literature, which was awarded to him in 1923.

The period following World War One saw the emergence of the modernist movement, its most famous exponent (in the field of poetry) being T. S. Eliot. Eliot wrote what is probably the most famous poem of the 20th century, *The Waste Land*, in 1922. Modernist poetry is often fragmented, unpredictable, and difficult, its form intended to capture and reflect the bewildering nature of modern experience.

As literature moves closer to us in time, it becomes harder to see particular patterns. But one way of reading later poets is in the light of the influence of earlier giants like Hardy and Eliot. Hardy's use of set verse forms is continued by W. H. Auden, best known for his poetry of the 1930s, which describe an uncertain period, with the next war looming. Like Hardy, Auden writes in a way which seems conversational and approachable, not deliberately obscure. Philip Larkin was also inspired by Hardy, capturing wry, rather downbeat experiences in rhymed and metrical verse forms. After him, James Fenton, Don Paterson, Glyn Maxwell and Simon Armitage are among those who have continued to use traditional verse to write about contemporary concerns.

The tradition of Modernism, on the other hand, has been continued

John Keats (1795 – 1821)

by writers like Basil Bunting, and later Geoffrey Hill, whose complex and demanding work records a tense and tough engagement with a range of issues, particularly our relationship to history.

Poetry today

At the start of the 21th century, with English established as a global language, the variety of cultures and identities to which English poetry gives expression has never been greater. We have already seen examples of this from Alice Oswald, and from the postcolonial writers, John Agard and Moniza Alvi. The work of the great Seamus Heaney, from its base in rural Northern Ireland, ranges over great territories of history, memory and experience. Recent poet laureates Andrew Motion and Carol Ann Duffy have been much concerned with introducing young people to poetry and making sure it has a place in normal lives. Poet-performers like Benjamin Zephaniah and Kate Tempest give poetry a vibrant place in public spaces. Poetry, in short, continues to speak to us in many tongues, and many voices.

DIFFERENT TYPES, OR GENRES, OF POETRY

1. Narrative Verse

Narrative verse tells stories: huge epic battles, small animal fables, folk ballads, nonsense tales, lays of ancient times, romances, tragedies. Once it was the mainstay of poetry. In ancient Athens, Homer's epic poems, *The Iliad* and *The Odyssey*, were at the centre of any educated person's view of the world. Chaucer's *Canterbury Tales*, and the contemporary *Sir Gawain and the Green Knight* are two of the chief glories of English medieval poetry, and great fun, too. (If the medieval language is an obstacle, try translations – Nevill Coghill's versions of Chaucer, Simon Armitage's rendering of *Gawain*.) The Elizabethans had Spenser's vast fantasy-verse-romance-allegory *The Faerie Queene* to enjoy. Two of the main types of narrative verse are the ballad and the epic; and we should look in on the dramatic monologue, too.

Ballad

The ballad, originating in oral tradition, is as much a sung as a spoken form. In a ballad, the narrative usually moves quickly, through a succession of boldly painted scenes. **Ballad metre** consists of a quatrain alternating iambic tetrameter and trimeter (4 beats, then 3 beats), and rhyming *abcb*.

> There lived a wife at Usher's Well,
>> And a wealthy wife was she;
> She had three stout and stalwart sons,
>> And sent them o'er the sea.

('The Wife of Usher's Well')

A ballad is usually impersonal: what matters is the tale, not the teller. And the tales often feature the adventures and wrongdoings of aristocrats and other posh folk, and heroic deeds by the common man. Broadside ballads provided subversive words which could be sung to well-known tunes (an art still practised by football fans). The ballad has been used as a vehicle to carry stories of battle, supernatural encounters, heroism, mystery and love.

In the eighteenth century, a renewed interest in folk heritage led to the collection of ballads in volumes such as Thomas Percy's *Reliques of Ancient English Poetry* (1765). This in turn influenced the *Lyrical Ballads* (1798) of Wordsworth and Coleridge, which aimed to recover the natural poetry of the popular voice, while at the same time employing the kind of irony and ambiguity which distinguishes the written literary tradition. Coleridge's 'The Ancient Mariner' is written in ballad metre, though with a more sophisticated thematic range than popular ballads. In the work of Bob Dylan (winner of the Nobel Prize for literature, let us remember) and other singers today, the ballad continues as a supple, expressive poetic form.

Epic

The epic takes us to the earliest, foundational stage of poetic history. An epic is an extended narrative, describing the feats of a heroic individual or tribe, whose actions are of momentous importance. The *Iliad* and *Odyssey*, both ascribed to the legendary Greek poet Homer, depict a warlike age and its values – courage, strength, ingenuity – and feature gods who quarrel amongst themselves and intervene in human affairs. Homer was imitated by the Roman poet Virgil, who used the epic form to describe the mythical founding of the Roman nation by Aeneas.

The Old English poem *Beowulf* describes the feats of its hero against monsters and a dragon, is also usually described as an epic. Written as early as 700AD, *Beowulf* gives us the fullest picture we are ever going to get of the grave, melancholy world of the Anglo-Saxons, their love of physical courage, sense of beauty – evident in the music of the verse itself – and awareness of the fragility of life.

In later English literature, the greatest epic work is Milton's *Paradise Lost* (1667). Milton set out to tell the story of Christianity and in doing so to outdo all previous epics in its scope, employing a style of intricate and daring baroque grandeur, with elaborate images tumbling through multi-rhythmed lines.

Some 19th-century poets undertook works of epic length, even if they cannot formally be called epics. William Wordsworth's The Prelude (written in 13 books in 1805, and published posthumously after a lifetime's tinkering in 1850) explores the growth of the poet's

T. S. Eliot (1888 – 1965)

mind, from his early tutoring by nature in Cumbria to the impressions of later life. Robert Browning's vast The Ring and the Book (1868) and here it takes 21,000 lines to deal with a 17th-century Italian murder trial.

The twentieth century brings T. S. Eliot's *The Waste Land* (1922). This gives us a vision of the inherited culture that made epic possible in fragments, like post-war rubble. From this point, high culture has seldom dared to reach towards the epic. But in popular culture, such as the Star Wars franchise, epic thrives and continues to thrill audiences with tales of gifted heroes performing great actions against mighty adversaries.

Dramatic Monologue

A dramatic monologue is a short narrative poem, which takes the form of a speech, or monologue, delivered by a speaker, who is clearly distinct from the author. It's something like a little one-man play. Robert Browning is particularly well known for his dramatic monologues: *The Ring and the Book*, mentioned above, is largely made up of them. In poems like 'Porphyria's Lover' and 'My Last Duchess', the speaker gives away things about himself and his subject, and part of the pleasure of reading is finding our way into the (sometimes very odd) mental state of the speaker. 'Porphyria's Lover' begins like this:

> The rain set early in tonight,
>   The sullen wind was soon awake,
> It tore the elm-tops down for spite,
>   And did its worst to vex the lake.
>   I listened with heart fit to break,
> When glided in Porphyria; straight
>   She shut the cold out and the storm …

At which point we might say 'Hold on! Who is this speaker, why is his heart breaking, and where is he? Why does he see Porphyria come in, without her seeing him?' 'Porphyria's Lover' prompts us to consider the kind of personality these thoughts may be coming from.

T. S. Eliot also uses the dramatic monologue in poems such as 'The Love Song of J Alfred Prufrock' (1915) and 'Gerontion' (1920), and though these are unlike Browning's poems in many ways, they still use the form to explore states of mind which seem broken, fragmented and mysterious:

> Here I am, an old man in a dry month,
> Being read to by a boy, waiting for rain.
> I was neither at the hot gates
> Nor fought in the warm rain
> Nor knee deep in the salt marsh, heaving a cutlass,
> Bitten by flies, fought.

('Gerontion')

A vivid emotional life is coming at us through these lines – the sensation of waiting, reflections on what the speaker did *not* do. (Is the boy reading him tales of ancient valour?) But the reflections are not necessarily the poet's. Eliot was an anti-romantic: he didn't want to write poems which were an outpouring of his own feelings. He felt that a good poem, like a well-made vase, should give pleasure even if we know nothing about the individual human being it comes from. So the form of the monologue suited Eliot's desire to keep the personality of the poet as much in the background as possible.

Story poems

Not all narrative verse is serious. There's the charming nonsense of Edward Lear's short *The Owl and the Pussycat* and Lewis Carroll's longer *The Hunting of the Snark*, or John Betjeman's evocative verse autobiography, *Summoned by Bells* (1960). And old material continues to be worked over and minted afresh: Derek Walcott's Caribbean epic

'Omeros' (1990) was inspired by Homer, while medieval narrative verse is itself enjoying a renaissance.

Recent years have given us Seamus Heaney's translations of *Beowulf* (1999) and the fables of the Scottish medieval poet Robert Henryson; Simon Armitage has produced a new, glowing version of the fourteenth-century *Sir Gawain and the Green Knight* (2009); Lavinia Greenlaw's *A Double Sorrow* (2014) is inspired by Chaucer's great verse romance *Troilus and Criseyde*. Patience Agbabi's *Telling Tales* (2015) is a compelling, funky remix of some of Chaucer's *Canterbury Tales*. These are tremendous places to start a poetry reading project, examples of how great poems, and great stories, speak across the ages.

2. Lyric

By far the most common kind of poetry today is so-called lyric poetry. At its best, a lyric poem compresses a memorable experience – be it a feeling, a thought, or an observation – into a compact form. Like this:

Ice Storm

Unable to sleep, or pray, I stand
by the window looking out
at moonstruck trees a December storm
has bowed with ice.

Maple and mountain ash bend
under its glassy weight,
their cracked branches falling upon
the frozen snow.

The trees themselves, as in winters past,
will survive their burdening,
broken thrive. And am I less to You,
my God, than they?

(Robert Hayden 1913-1980)

Twelve lines. Less than a minute to read aloud. Yet after those twelve short lines we may feel that we, and the world, have, in some way, changed. The smallest moments can tell the greatest stories. Here, a situation we can recognise – standing by the window at night – leads us, by soft, quiet steps, from precise observations to a meditation on time and suffering and faith. The abstract is grounded in the concrete.

The poem is a masterpiece of lyric economy. Try taking a word out, or changing one, without losing the final effect. It can't be done. The specific images, the particularising adjectives – *moonstruck trees, glassy weight* – make the moment so real, so tangible, that for the minute of the poem we *become* the speaker, unable to sleep, or pray, even if we haven't prayed in years, or even thought of doing so. William Blake wrote of the ability to "To see a World in a Grain of Sand". This poem aims at something similar.

And we can be moved by it without knowing anything about the speaker. It wasn't until years after coming across this poem that I learned Hayden was an African American, and wondered whether the burdened trees of 'Ice Storm' might be an image for the burdens of his own people.

The lyric voice

In reading lyric poetry, we need to think about the "I" speaking. Sometimes it may suggest powerfully the autobiographical voice of the poet, as in Hardy's *Poems of 1912 –13*, in which the poet remembers his dead wife. In other cases the "I" may be a voice devised for this particular poem: we do not know whether Shakespeare's sonnets have any autobiographical content at all, for example. And even the "I" of the most ardently personal poem may to some extent be devised for the text, and not have a one-to-one identity with the author. We tend to refer to "the speaker" when discussing a lyric, the voice that's created for this poem, this moment.

Let us look briefly now at some of the chief kinds of lyric.

Elegy

An elegy is a poem lamenting the death of a loved one or public figure and reflecting on serious themes. Milton's *Lycidas* (1637) establishes a tradition of **pastoral elegy**, in which a figure is mourned in a long meditative poem using pastoral imagery of nymphs, satyrs and the countryside. Later examples include Gray's *Elegy Written in a Country Churchyard* (1751), which contemplates the passage of human life and the passing of time. Shelley's *Adonais* (1821) on the death of Keats, is also a vision of the nature of poetry.

Tennyson's *In Memoriam A.H.H.* (1850) records the intense private thoughts of the poet on the loss of a close friend. W. H. Auden's *In Memory of W B Yeats* (1939) is an example of an elegy on a public figure which embraces serious wider themes, such as the place of poetry in society. The term has been generally applied to anything with a melancholy or plaintive mood, which can be labelled **elegiac**.

Elegies continue to be a mainstay of the lyric tradition. At their centre is an evocation of love and loss which we can hold up against our own, like a candle in the dark. Northern Irish poets Seamus Heaney, Derek Mahon and Michael Longley have all written elegies as powerful as any in the language. Among them, this:

Marigolds, 1960

You are dying. Why do we fight?
You find my first published poem -
'Not worth the paper it's printed on,'
You say. She gave him marigolds -

You are dying. 'They've cut out my
Wheesht - I have to sit down
To wheesht - like a woman' -
Marigolds the colour of autumn –

I need to hitchhike to Dublin
For Trinity Term. 'I'll take you
Part of the way,' you say
Again and again, and in pain.

And we talk and talk as though
We know we are just in time.
'A little bit further,' you say
Again and again, and in pain.

A few miles from Drogheda
You turn the car. We say goodbye
And you drive away slowly
Towards Belfast and your death.

To keep in his cold room. Look
At me now on the Newry Road
Standing beside my rucksack. Och,
Daddy, look in your driving mirror.

It is hard to explain the power of this poem, but we can note some of its elements – the simple, direct language, for example. The tense is what a trained classicist like Michael Longley would call the past perfect: the present describing an event in the past, to capture it in its vivid details. There is no asking for sympathy. And the emotions – love, fear, grief – are all the more powerful because they are not stated directly. The poem evokes the way we try to hold feelings at bay. And it reminds us that the deepest feelings often find the simplest language:

> And we talk and talk as though
> We know we are just in time.

Ode

The word 'ode' has a rather musty air. I am not sure that many contemporary poets have composing an ode on their to-do lists. But some of the greatest poems in the language have been odes. Originally, it was a poem of praise, employed by the ancient Greek poet Pindar to celebrate (with music) the victors of the Olympic games; and it was also employed for quieter ruminations by the Roman poet Horace (see the marvellous translations by David West).

In English literature, odes were especially popular between about 1750 and 1900, which was roughly when the craze for all things classical was at its height. Writers associated the form with complex and varying stanza forms, with shifting metre. The Romantics wrote odes to convey the feeling of an exploratory passage of thought. Examples: Wordsworth, 'Ode: Intimations of Immortality', Keats, 'Ode on a Grecian Urn'.

3. The Sonnet

English poems come in all shapes and sizes, from little couplets to vast epics.

Some forms suit certain kinds of material: the ballad is handy for telling stories; blank verse (unrhymed iambic pentameter), with its room for varied sentences and speech rhythms, suits the dramatic poetry of Shakespeare.

One form which keeps coming up in English verse is the 14-line sonnet. Imported from Italy in the 16th century, this became the verse form of choice for many love poets. A little too long for a short lyrical outburst, but a little too short for a story, the sonnet seems perfect for a little internal drama, a thought going for a walk.

There are two main kinds of sonnet, the Italian and the English. The Italian sonnet divides into an **octave** (a group of eight lines) which rhymes *abbaabba*, and a **sestet** (six lines) which makes various patterns out of *cde* rhymes. The point where the octave meets the sestet is called the **volta**, meaning 'turn', and it is often here that the sonnet 'turns' by taking us in a new direction. Here is an example:

> Remember me when I am gone away,
>> Gone far away into the silent land;
>> When you can no more hold me by the hand,
> Nor I half turn to go yet turning stay.
> Remember me when no more day by day
>> You tell me of our future that you planned:
>> Only remember me; you understand
> It will be late to counsel then or pray.
> Yet if you should forget me for a while
>> And afterwards remember, do not grieve:
>> For if the darkness and corruption leave
>> A vestige of the thoughts that once I had,

Better by far you should forget and smile
Than that you should remember and be sad.

(Christina Rossetti 1830-1894)

This poem packs a powerful punch in a short space: it's like a voice from the grave, allowing the bereaved to "move on" and be happy. And it gains part of its power from being very tightly organised. That tightness adds to its intensity.

We notice that the octave divides clearly into two **quatrains**, each ending in a full stop. The first quatrain says:

Remember me when I'm not here any more.

And the second is a variation on that:

Remember me when I'm not here to speak to.

We notice, too, that the lines are largely end-stopped: the speaker is firmly in control of what she is saying. The form demands control: that *abbaabba* is a tough discipline, requiring the poet to find four *a* and four *b* sounds, without any of them appearing forced. That's much harder to do in English than Italian.

After line eight comes the **volta**, and here we get a signal of a new direction with the word *Yet*, followed by the reassuring message that it's all right to forget sometimes, that the main thing is to hold on to what was good, and to be happy rather than permanently mournful: *Remember me... but* is the basic outline of the argument.

The rhyme scheme for the sestet here is *cddece*. The six lines follow a line of thought as it works itself out in the last line and concludes with the third and last full stop of the poem. The Italian sonnet is sometimes also called the Petrarchan sonnet, because it was much used by the medieval Italian poet Petrarch, particularly famous for his love sonnets: it is as if the stern demands of the form make a suitably sturdy container for the simmering contents.

The English sonnet also has an octave and a sestet, but the rhyme scheme is different: *ababcdcdefefgg*. Seven rhyme sounds, rather than five, with none needed more than twice. This form is also called the Shakespearean sonnet, as it's particularly associated with him. So let's take an example from Shakespeare. Here he is making fun of the kind of love sonnets that were fashionable at the time, with their lavish praise – in imitation of Petrarch – of the lady's beauties:

> My mistress' eyes are nothing like the sun;
> Coral is far more red than her lips' red;
> If snow be white, why then her breasts are dun;
> If hairs be wires, black wires grow on her head.
> I have seen roses damask'd, red and white,
> But no such roses see I in her cheeks;
> And in some perfumes is there more delight
> Than in the breath that from my mistress reeks:
> I love to hear her speak, yet well I know
> That music hath a far more pleasing sound;
> I grant I never saw a goddess go,
> My mistress when she walks treads on the ground.
> > And yet by heaven I think my love as rare
> > As any she belied with false compare.

Again we have a full stop or heavy pause at the end of each quatrain of the octave. The octave is made up of short sentences (unlike Rossetti's): the first four end-stopped lines are all complete clauses. Over these eight lines, Shakespeare is really repeating, with variations, a single idea: *my* beloved is nothing like these ridiculous idealised pictures you read about.

We then expect the volta, but there is no "turn" here. The poet simply continues the same line of thought: *her* breath isn't like music, and she doesn't float like a goddess.

This is quite common in the English sonnet: instead of octave and sestet we get three quatrains (*ababcdcdefef*) leading to a final **rhyming couplet**. And it's here that we find the volta, signalled by the same word Rossetti used: *And yet*. We've been kept waiting for that *yet* over 12 lines. The couplet here means:

> *I think my love's as precious as any woman who is lied about with false comparisons (any she means any woman)*

The couplets at the end of Shakespeare's sonnets are put to all sorts of uses, from the delayed volta here, to a concluding nugget of proverbial wisdom. The Romantic poet John Keats preferred the Italian sonnet because he thought the English one was weighed down by that last couplet. On the other hand, there's always the danger that the Italian sonnet, with its strict octave rhyme scheme, can sound a little stiff.

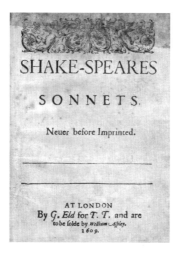